EST. 2012

BLACK **B&W** WHITE

PALETTE

№1

New Monochrome
Graphics

by

Viction:ary

&Larry | + Ruddigkeit | 10inc. | A3 Collectif | Acne JR | Alex Dalmau | Alexander Kent | ART+COM | ARTIVA DESIGN | Asylum | Atelier BangBang | Atelier Christian von der Heide | Atipus | BERG | Berger & Föhr | BLOW | Bravo&Tango | Brogen Averill | Bunch | C100 Purple Haze | Campaign | Case Studyo | Caserne | Cesar Del Valle | Coco | COMMUNE | Company | Craig & Karl | Damien Poulain | DEMIAN CONRAD DESIGN | dn&co. | Edited | Emily Forgot | Emmanuel Bossuet | Esther Stocker | FEB Design | FEIXEN: Design by Felix Pfäffli | FIBA Design | filthymedia | Fons Hickmann m23 | Francesc Moret Vayreda | Graphic design studio by Yurko Gutsulyak | Greece is for Lovers | Happycentro | HelloMe | Here Design | Hovercraft Studio | Ibán Ramón + Dídac Ballester | ilovedust | Information Architects | Jan Eumann | Joan Ramon Pastor | Johanna Bonnevier | John Barton | Jordan Metcalf | Josip Kelava | Kasper Pyndt Studio | Larissa Kasper and Rosario Florio | Lava | Leterme Dowling | Lívia Hasenstaub | Lo Siento | Lotta Nieminen | Mads Jakob Poulsen | Marie-Niamh Dowling | Mark Brooks Graphik Design | Maximo Riera | Michael Garrett | Michael Hansen | Michael Johansson | Miklós Ferencz | Morey Talmor | Murmure | nendo | NOMO Design | Non-Format | Not Available | POKETO | POOL | Raffinerie AG für Gestaltung | Root | Rui Ribeiro | ruiz+company | Smel | Stewart Walker | Studio Astrid Stavro | Studio Marcus Kraft | STUDIO NEWWORK | STUDIOLAV | StudioMakgill | Tadas Karpavičius | The Hello Poster Show | Therese Sennerholt Design | This Studio | Todd Borka | Tokyo-Go-Go Illustration Studio | TOYKYO | Wang Zhi Hong | Wudai Shiguo

Palette 01:

BLACK & WHITE
New Monochrome Graphics

Published and distributed by
viction workshop ltd

viction workshop ltd
Unit C, 7/F, Seabright Plaza, 9-23 Shell Street,
North Point, Hong Kong
Url: www.victionary.com Email: we@victionary.com
www.facebook.com/victionworkshop
www.twitter.com/victionary_
www.weibo.com/victionary

Edited and produced by viction:ary

Concepts & art direction by Victor Cheung
Book design by viction workshop ltd

Fourth Edition
©2012, 2013, 2014, 2016 viction workshop ltd
Copyright on text and design work is held by respective
designers and contributors.

ISBN 978-988-19439-5-8
Printed and bound in China

EST. 2012

BLACK **B&W** WHITE

PALETTE

№ 1

New Monochrome
Graphics

by

Viction:ary

black and white are not colours— they are philosophies. The fact that black and white both refuse to be defined as colours is part of their political agenda.

But let's begin by concentrating on colour theory and examining the particular media that designers work with. First off is the additive colour system used for producing printed material. By overprinting a few— generally four— transparent inks, we can create countless different colour tones. If all four colours are printed on top of each other, the result is a deep black. But before designers get to the printing stage, they normally develop their ideas on a computer screen. And here, everything is the other way round. Computer monitors work with light. On screen, only three colours are relevant. And when these overlap, the result is a dazzling white.

Black and white are condensed information— information that is communicated through colour. Compressed inside black and white is total information. Black and white are the product, the sum of all information.

If we accept this principle, we soon realise that black and white can no longer be described as monochromatic. In fact they're omnichromatic. Nothing is more diverse than black and white. Everything else is just brightly coloured. And however brilliant the brightly coloured may sometimes appear, they always contain a lim-

ited number of colours and a finite amount of information. Brightly coloured is measurable. Black and white are infinite.

The sheer immeasurability of black and white, combined with the way they escape rigid classification, contains a provocative element. They fuel paranoia about the rising forces of subversion and anarchy. They spread fear— the writer's terror when facing the ghostly white of blank pages, the anxiety encountered by a film director when confronting the blackness of the empty screen, the military fear of white flags, the dread amongst politicians of a mental blackout.

But hope picks up at the sight of white bridal gowns and black underwear. Oil is "black gold" — sold by men in white robes to dealers with bank accounts in the black. We are sucked towards black holes and pray for immaculate conception. Doves and angels shimmer before our eyes while we seek the path of enlightenment in the blackness of night.

Black and white are dialectic principles. On the one hand, we can achieve total density by compressing information into them. On the other hand, we can extrapolate any information we want back out of them. And because black and white encompass everything, they provide the ideal surface for projecting ideas onto and interpreting things out of. Black and white are realms of the imagination, kingdoms of the subconscious, countries rich in hopes and dreams.

Which is why I look forward to a future when all televisions, cinema screens, advertising displays and computer monitors are white. And all newspapers, posters and books are black.

...tion:ary

viction workshop ltd
Unit C, 7/F, Seabright Plaza,
North Point, Hong Kong
Url: www.victionary.com   Em
www.facebook.com/viction
www.twitter.com/victionary
www.weibo.com/victionary

Edited and produced by viction:ar

Concepts & art direction by Victor Che
Book design by viction workshop ltd

Fourth Edition
©2012, 2013, 2014, 2016 viction workshop ltd
Copyright on text and design work is held by respective
designers and contributors.

ISBN 978-988-19439-5-8
Printed and bound in China

"Black and white are realms of the imagination, kingdoms of the subconscious, countries rich in hopes and dreams."

—

Prof. Fons Hickmann

"If you can make the message come across in your design by using black and white only, then everything else is just decoration."
—

Johanna Bonnevier

Edited

Concept
Book des

Fourth Edi
©2012, 2013
Copyright or
designers and

The use of black and white in graphics and text goes back a long way in time, and maybe this is one of the reasons why we continue to come back to it. It is familiar and traditional, yet so basic that it can be used in new contemporary context and compositions without the connotations of tradition and past times.

These two basic colours are the default in almost all situations, from pen and paper to modern computer programs. With the birth of colour photography most photographers photograph in colour today, yet many writers, designers and the like choose to stick with using black and white as their main direction. How come we don't want to present the world as we know it (it is after all a very colourful place)? Maybe we are using abstraction as a means to achieve greater clarity.

In most places where we see monochrome design, it has been implemented for obvious reasons. Film credits are, for example, very rarely in any other colours as we need the strong contrast between black and white to make the small words legible, as they can often be displayed in low resolution as well. The strong contrast makes it perfect for perception in bad lighting condition, in small type, on screen... the list goes on, yet many designers like to keep to black and white in other occasions as well. So what is it that we find so intriguing and interesting with black and white? Colour tends to go in trends, whilst black and white graphics have proven to withstand the test of time much better. Perhaps just because as previously mentioned, that it is so basic and familiar. Going back to basics and cutting all other colours out also allow for a stronger focus on the composition or shape in the design, and maybe the message as well.

One can argue that if you can make the message come across in your design by using black and white only, then everything else is just decoration. Other colours come with many different connotations depending on where you are in the world, whilst black and white are more neutral and less infected with presumptions. With this in mind it does come clear why this would be the safe choice for any multinational design piece. Black and white design are not completely spared from connotations though. The most common reflections that come to mind whilst discussing this subject are innocence, elegance, economy, cleanness, simpleness or sophistication. As with any design, how you respond to it depends so much more than just on the choice of colours used, although this has of course its play in it as well. It is in the eyes of the beholder, we just need to find as much common ground as possible for the target group to react on.

Looking forward, it will be interesting to see if we think of colour (in general and of course black and white in particular) in the same way as we now do. Technology makes it easier for us to implement more and more colours into design every day. Web-based graphics are restricted by the screen on which they are displayed, but the technology in this is rapidly evolving. Printed graphics have also changed drastically with new technology in the last decades. With digital printing pushing the envelope each day, one of the latest being the ability to print white colour. Will the availability and easy access to colour numb our sense of its usage, or will we embrace it and thus replace black and white with a more colourful spectra?

Foreword

There is magic in black and white. Its simplicity allows us to make instantaneous connections. Even from birth, as our blurry sight develops, this duality offers the maximum contrast we need to distinguish forms in the world around us. Our brains are hard-wired to recognise this distinct colour relationship. From the most humble of yard sale signs and lost-and-found flyers, to the most elegant and scrutinised corporate logo, this dynamic palette offers a no-frills sense of authenticity. It is a great equaliser in the world of art and design, allowing form and content to lead the way in any medium.

In the loud and fast landscape of visual culture, colour is abundant. Your latest retina screen offers a digital paradise of hues. And long gone are the days when the cost of full colour printing was set at a premium price. With all the calibrations under the rainbow at your fingertips, it is not hard to see why a return to simple black and white would be a refreshing palette to designers.

When we decided to limit The Hello Poster Show's Lost+Found edition to black and white, we were certain it would offer a level of sophistication and intrigue no other colour combination could offer. Our previous shows had employed a bright pop of red, a hip shade of aubergine, and a rich cyan. But what if we built a show on the bare bones palette of black and white? No other palette ever fit so perfectly into the 'less is more' mantra we employ as we curate and develop new shows. Our call for entries prompted our community of designers and art-

ists to create a silkscreen poster embodying the theme of Lost+Found with only black paper and white ink. It was a challenge for our designers and artists to rely on form and contrast alone to get the job done. This stark colour palette allowed form to dictate the composition, making for straightforward, elegant pieces. The success of the show was proof enough of the impact of this dynamic colour duo.

Even in our individual careers, limiting the colour palette to black and white is a standard practice in the first phases of a project. Narrowing the options and setting such guidelines let us (and our clients) focus on form and content without the distraction of delectable RGB and CMYK palettes. In that sense, it's a very freeing palette to work in, even if the end result embraces a full spectrum of hues and tones. Without the aid of colour, we are often able to come up with more creative and intriguing solutions that may have never been explored otherwise.

A quote from Paul Graham says, "When you're forced to be simple, you're forced to face the real problem. When you can't deliver ornament, you have to deliver substance." Working in a world of solely black and white will certainly challenge you to deliver substance, and act as a leverage point for drama, dynamism and simplicity.

"Working in a world of solely black and white will certainly challenge you to deliver substance, and act as a leverage point for drama, dynamism and simplicity."

—

Alanna MacGowan + Benjamin K. Shown

Tadas

Designer's personal business cards.
His creeds of design were visually
inscribed in the minimal colours
and unorthodox triangular shape ac-
cented by structural line patterns.

Tadas Karpavičius

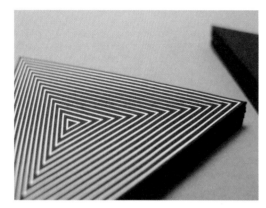

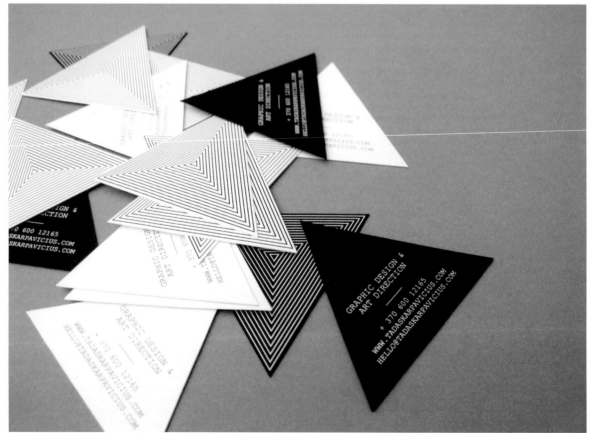

Typographic Sliding Puzzles

A playful way to display the beauty of letterforms. Each puzzle features one alphabet in a distinctive style and accents letterforms in both a logical and abstract way.

Stewart Walker

"We live in colours. Being monochromatic is a distinction, however."

The Full Moon Mission

Given out to clients during the Moon Festival, these mooncakes were an entreaty for creative revolutions, like how Chinese revolutionists used to orchestrate revolts. The gift referenced the company's name, which literally refers to the era of political turmoil in ancient China.

Wudai Shiguo

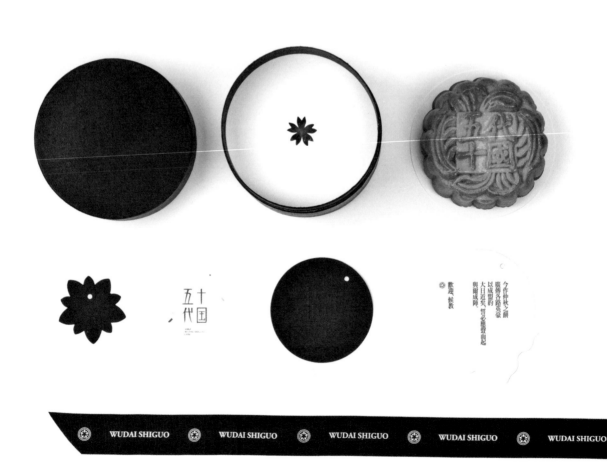

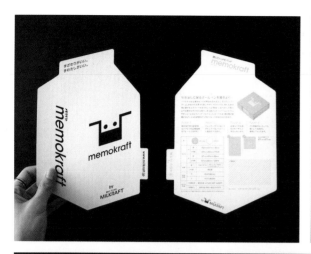

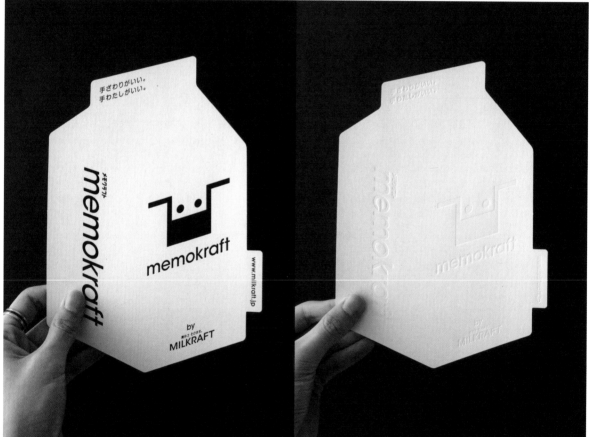

Milkraft

Branding and identity for Milkraft, who recycles milk
cartons to manufacture paper and paper packaging. The
logo is a marriage of cow and cardbox, with emphases on
the natural, rustic quality remained in their products.

COMMUNE, Futaba

Copywriting: Kosuke Ikehata
Photo: Sukehiro Nakamura
Client: Morita

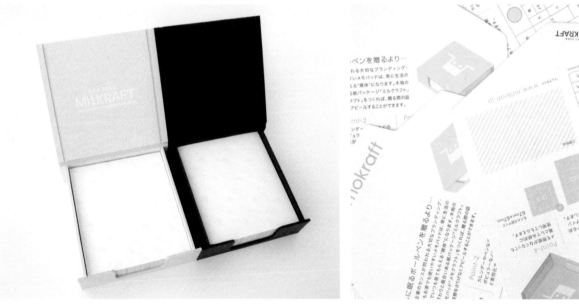

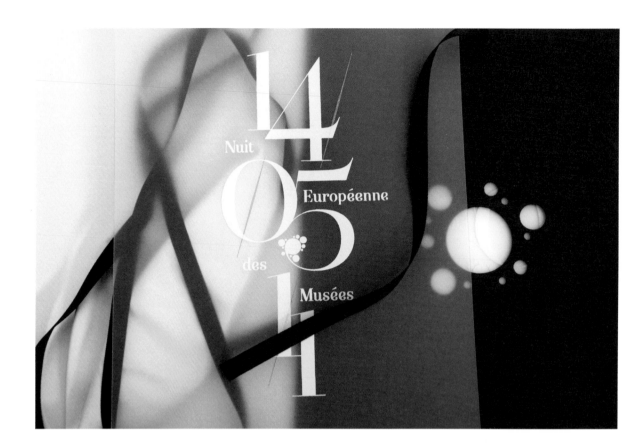

Musée des Beaux-Arts de Caen

European Museums Night

Street-marketing concept aimed to lure visitors to discover a luminous and ethereal installation at European Night of Museums 2011. Invitation cards were sent down the town in black envelopes held by glowing balloons in the dark.

Murmure

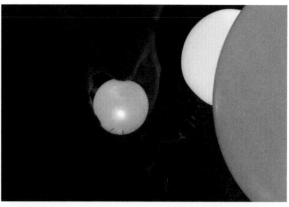

Flavour of the Month

Packaging for a delicious-looking paper-weight in the form of a white marble ice pop with a chromed brass stick.

Company
Photo/ client: Greece is for Lovers

あす9月4日（土）ルイ・ヴィトン 名古屋栄店 リニューアルオープン

Shinsaibashi Plaza bldg 1F 3-12-12 Minami Senba Chuo-ku, Osaka   www.louisvuitton.com

LOUIS VUITTON

LV Origami Invitation

Invitation for the opening of Louis Vuitton's new store in Osaka, Japan. The extension of Happycentro's paper sculptures accentuated the idea of perpetual precision and pureness in delicate folds, accurate calculations and special printing techniques.

Happycentro

Client: Louis Vuitton

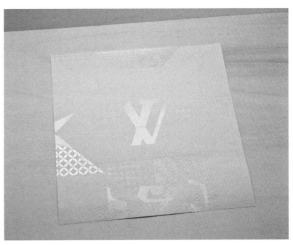

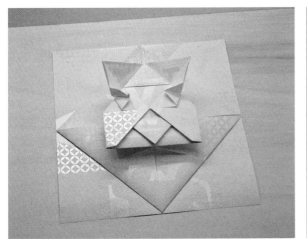

Beyond Dessert Packaging

Retail packaging for Beyond Dessert's often lavishly-
decorated bite-sized cakes. By leaving enormous
open space above the rack, the carrier offers
customers a comfortable grip, as well as generous
protection and display for the lovely CakePops.

BLOW
Client: Beyond Dessert

Celebrate Audio's Birthday & Housewarming

Bespoke invitations to Audio Brighton's turning-six party held in conjunction with the opening of their Southampton branch. The six hovering circles emblematic of its disco theme were foil-stamped, debossed and triplexed by Generation Press.

filthymedia

Client: Audio Brighton, Audio Southampton

"Printing black on black and white on white always give a classic feel."

_dio's 6th Birthday

_obile Disco (Dj Set)
_tember
_rom 10pm
_ Admits two
_een 10–11pm drinks £1

_anking you all for your
_ontinued support

Audio
10 Marine Parade
Brighton
audiobrighton.com

—— Celebrate Audio's 6th Birthday

—— Simian Mobile Disco (Dj Set)
17th September
Arrive from 10pm
Invite Admits two
Between 10–11pm drinks £1

—— Thanking you all for your
continued support

—— Audio
10 Marine Parade
Brighton
audiobrighton.com

—— Celebrate Audio's Housewarming

—— Foamo, Cagedbaby and Last Japan
18th September at 10pm
Invite Admits two

—— Audio
5–6a Waterloo Terrace
Southampton
SO15 2AL
audiosouthampton.com
02380 630171

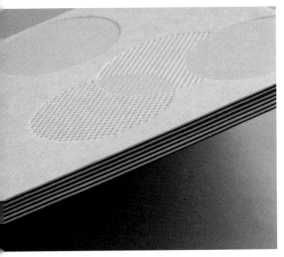

PURPOSE OF USE

As an aid to reduce illicit
opioid use and for the relief o
opioid withdrawl symptoms

Keep out of the reach of child

Store at room temperature 13.30
Read enclosed leaflet before u

HABTT

HABIT

Branding and packaging for drug cessation
products manufactured by Habit Pharmaceu-
ticals. From methadone and nicotine patches
to users' pamphlets, the approach ensures
rehabilitation can be a luxurious, exclusive
and discreet experience too.

Morey Talmor

TA—CD

Nicocettine 0.4ml

HABTT

RX only

METHADONE

METHADONE HYDROCHLORIDE

250ml

RX only   HABTT

IBOGAINE

Tabernanthe iboga 1gr   RX only

HABTT

SUBOXONE

BUPRENORPHINE 2mg

NALAXONE 0.5mg

HABTT

RX only   30 tablets

Playground Plates

Illustrations on ceramic plates specially produced for group exhibition, 6 Impossible Things To Do Before Breakfast. The collection included curious acts, such as riding a bird with a knife, holding people in a cage and rowing a shoe.

Emily Forgot

"I love the simplicity and economy of design in black and white."

Mori Mini Cup

Original designs by late Japanese ceramic designer, Masahiro Mori. POKETO retails the mini cups which can serve sake and spirits or as decorative display.

Masahiro Mori
Retail: POKETO

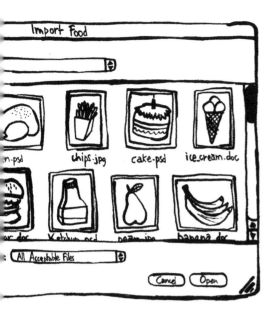

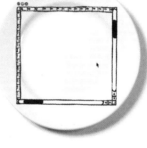

iPlate

Plate set metaphorically comparing the nature of cooking with photo-editing work. All sorts of familiar photo-editing buttons and cursor were illustrated at the brim of the plates, while food could remain in the limelight.

Todd Borka

Amen Tableware

Side plates and dinner plates, with
an 'A' from the word 'amen' to project
the popular rebellious sentiment of
modern Greeks.

Greece is for Lovers

Photo: Nikos Alexolpoulos

Archeology

China plates and cups as a reflection on how crafts and objects could be interpreted in the digital age. The larger collection follows the same principle with 3D renderings on the theme of diet.

STUDIOLAV, Marc Schulthess

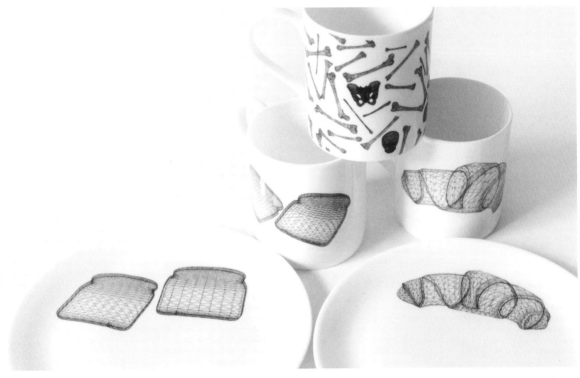

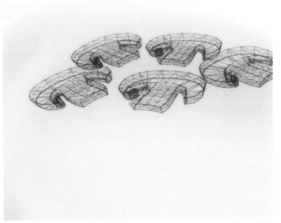

Jean Pierre Le Douche

Like a black-spotted poodle walking on heels, this graceful porcelain creature with golden eyes is produced with an edition of 25. It impressively measures 45cm tall, 55cm long by 22cm wide and retails in a silk-screened wooden case.

Parra

Production: Case Studyo

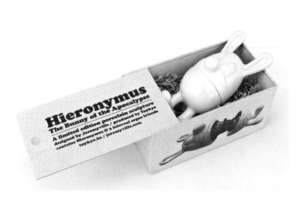

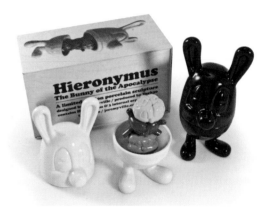

TOYKYO x Artists

You & I by Steven Harrington; and, on facing page, *Hieronymus: The Bunny of the Apocalypse* by Jeremyville. The limited edition glazed porcelain figures are art collaborations between artists and TOYKYO. Each comes in a wooden box with the sculptures' screenprint and artist's signature.

Steven Harrington, Jeremyville
Production: TOYKYO

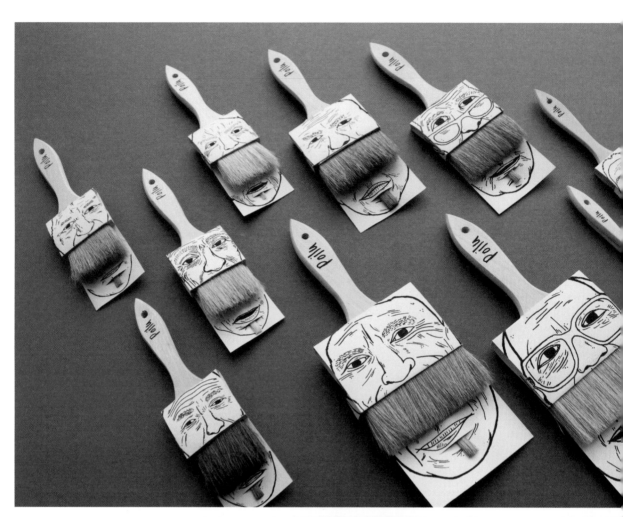

Poilus

Paper packaging that turns paintbrush
sets into an old man with trimmed beard
and a big moustache. The brushes are
identified by names and size numbers.
The wrapper doubles as a rest to dry a wet
brush's paint.

Atelier BangBang

*Special credits: Professor Sylvain Allard,
Université du Québec à Montréal (UQAM)*

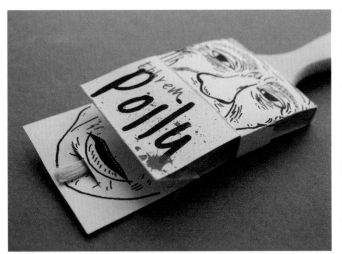

Triticum

Takeaway packaging for Xevi Ramon's craft work, with a goal to aschew all kinds of glue and industrial process in its production. Squid ink was used for printing to complement the breads' authentic rural flavour and the baker's concept.

Lo Siento
Client: Triticum

La Main - Bagel Co.

Packaging for Montreal bagel maker named after St. Laurent street's nickname. The locale's historical values and the bagels' unique wood-fired baked nature converge on a vintage map wrapper, sealed with stickers indicating history and the content of the pack.

Caserne

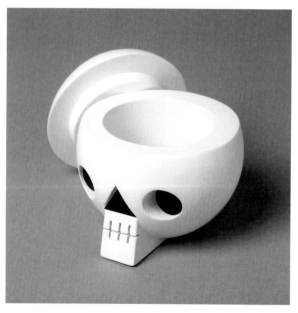

Kranium

Wooden skull with a removable cranium and secret compartment for treasures and memories. The skull is delivered in a cardboard box with a graphic *Kranium* print.

Acne JR

Chester

Swedish teddy bear made from artificial leather and eco-friendly rayon filling. Comes with an address label and a storage bag with a graphic *Chester* print.

Acne JR

Acne JR
Packaging

Cardboard boxes and storage bags for Acne JR's toys. Each features a graphic depiction of the toy it contains.

Acne JR

A3 collectif Business Card

A3, being a group with diverse talents for strategic communication and graphic design, is made direct and clear on their business cards. Simply silkscreened in white over black, each of the four symbols represents a staff member of A3.

A3 Collectif

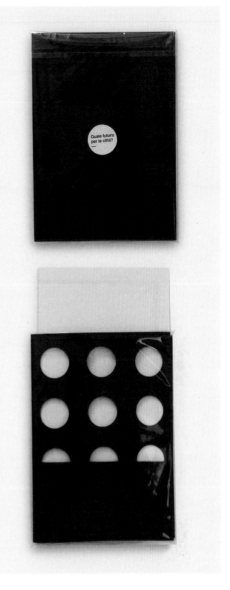

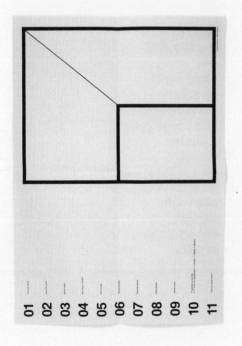

Quale Futuro Per La Città?

Folders, poster and packaging for a lecture series with focuses on the city's future and architects' role in it. The windows constituted a subtle hint at the profession and connoted the architects' clear and open vision over the town.

ARTIVA DESIGN
Client: OBR Open Building Research (Plug_in)

JOC de Jordi Oliver Conti

JOC is Catalan for "Play". By leaving windows on the label, the graphic system leads to three whites in a row and win a tic-tac-toe game as drinkers down the wine.

Francesc Moret Vayreda

Client: Jordi Oliver Conti
Special credits: Carlota Oliver

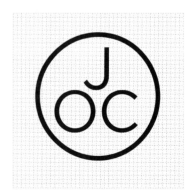

The Catmonger

Handpainted wood sculpture exclusively crafted to partake in a group show about furniture design. The cat measures 45cm tall and 30cm wide with an edition of one.

Damien Poulain

Aloja Negre Wine

Distinct with a Mediterranean character and prevalence of balsamic, Aloja was named after the Catalan sea goddess who is energic but tender. The lengthy, sinuous hair of Aloja creates a sense of mystery as it twines around the bottle.

Atipus

Illustration: Oriol Malet
Client: Celler Coca i Fitó

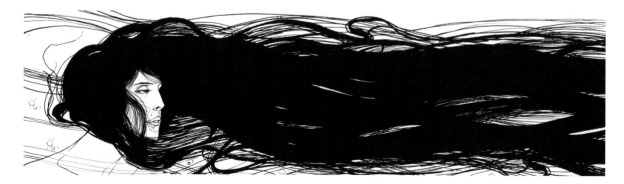

Schepps Dairy Rebranding

New packaging to tell Schepps, the long-established Texas dairy product brand, anew after recently bought out. The design introduces a new skim milk line, *Superior*, with infused flavours, such as lavender and cinnamon.

Michael Garrett

Good Day Milk

Sold as a limited product to raise fund for Japan, Good Day Milk reminds people of "good things (white space) will come around after the bad (black spots)". Naturally, the bottle is also a refreshing edition of a cow's brindle.

Not Available

Client: Good Day

"Black and white can convey an infinite variety of emotions, from elation to desperation. Monotonous? We think not."

Narvik & Pinvin

Traditional knitting patterns to dress up smartphones, with hints of the British and Norwegian origins of the designers of Non-Format.

Non-Format
Client: AU (KDDI)

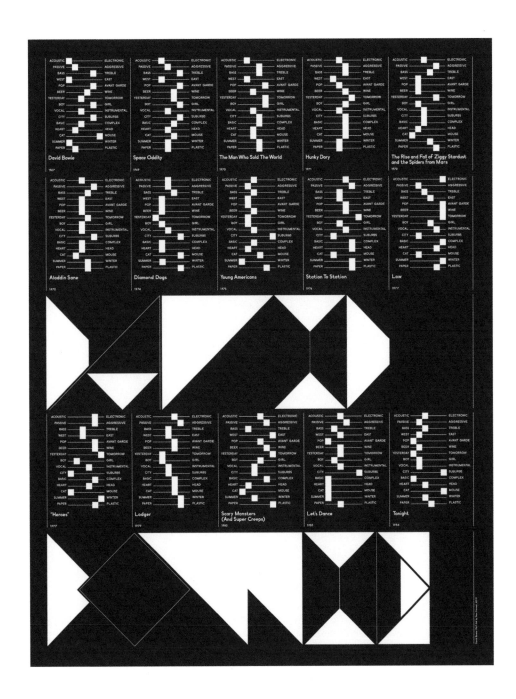

David Bowie 1967–84

Poster for UK? OK!!, an exhibition of British graphics at
Parco Factory, Tokyo. Mixers and sliders were deliberately
positioned to describe Bowie's albums, with inspirations
from the notions of Axis Thinking by Brian Eno.

Non-Format

Client: Parco Factory

No Sleep Till Hades

Merchandise playing on the belief that can be literally interpreted as "stay awake until death". Hades is the underworld and god of death in Greek myth.

Greece is for Lovers
Photo: Eleanna Kokkini

Lisez-moi
Counter-Print.co.uk

Lees Mij
Counter-Print.co.uk

Read Me
Counter-Print.co.uk

Leggimi
Counter-Print.co.uk

Counter-Print.co.uk
International Online Print Sellers
Books/Magazines/Journals/Ephemera
Photography/Architecture/Product Design/
Art/Graphic Design/Typography/Illustration

Counter-Print.co.uk
International Online
Print Sellers
Books
Magazines
Journals
Ephemera
Photography
Architecture
Product Design
Art
Graphic Design
Typography
Illustration

Counter-Print.co.uk
International Online
Print Sellers
Books
Magazines
Journals
Ephemera
Photography
Architecture
Product Design
Art
Graphic Design
Typography
Illustration

Counter-Objects.co.uk
International Online
Design Shop
Posters
Lighting
Furniture
Clothing
Stationery
Photography
Product Design
Fashion Design
Art
Graphic Design
Typography
Illustration

Eight:48
International Design
Magazine
Photography
Product Design
Fashion
Art
Graphic Design
Typography
Illustration
Web
www.eight48.com

Counter-Print

Brand identity, website and marketing materials for Counter-Print, an online book store for vintage art and design books. Helvetica was used as the primary font with a rigid grid system to hold everything together.

Leterme Dowling

Illustration: (Poster) Robert Hanson, (Bag, Bookmark) Anthony Burrill
Client: Counter-Print

Counter-Print.co.uk

You've
Got Mail (1)

Counter-
Print.co.uk

International
Online Print
Sellers

This voucher is redeemable for the
amount of £10 at www.counter-print.co.uk
For use, email info@counter-print.co.uk
with your choice of items, quoting the code:

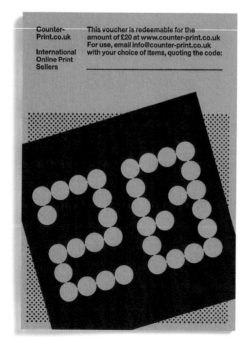

Counter-
Print.co.uk

International
Online Print
Sellers

This voucher is redeemable for the
amount of £20 at www.counter-print.co.uk
For use, email info@counter-print.co.uk
with your choice of items, quoting the code:

Counter-
Print.co.uk

International
Online Print
Sellers

This voucher is redeemable for the
amount of £50 at www.counter-print.co.uk
For use, email info@counter-print.co.uk
with your choice of items, quoting the code:

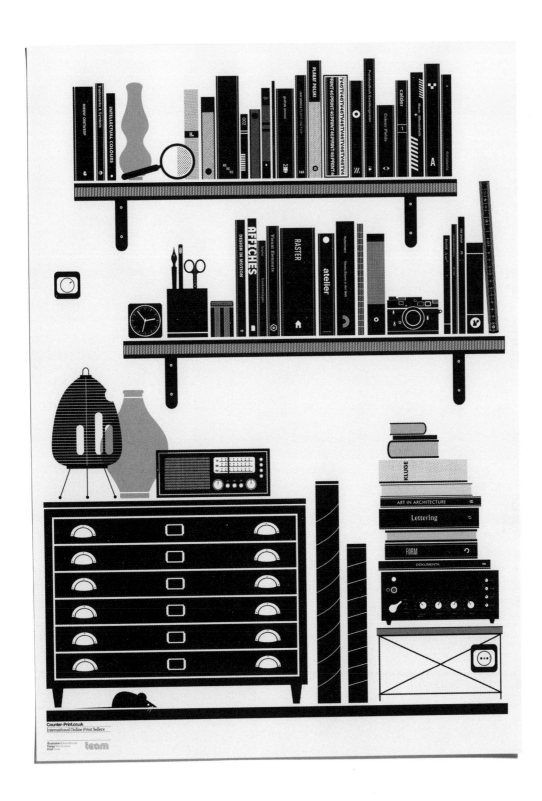

"Black and white suit our bold graphics and are visually more powerful and cost effective at the same time."

Signal No.1

Special edition tote bag and postcard to celebrate BLOW's first anniversary. Typhoon warning Standby Signal No.1 was borrowed to compare BLOW's emergence as an approaching tropical cyclone to watch out.

BLOW

Le Manoir

Packaging for a new luxury cream formulated by dermatologist, Dr. Peter Kessler, based on in-depth personal skin analysis. Black and white communicate pure essence, where the red wax seal creates a rupture against rationality in this product.

Atelier Christian von der Heide

Client: Dr. med. Peter Kessler

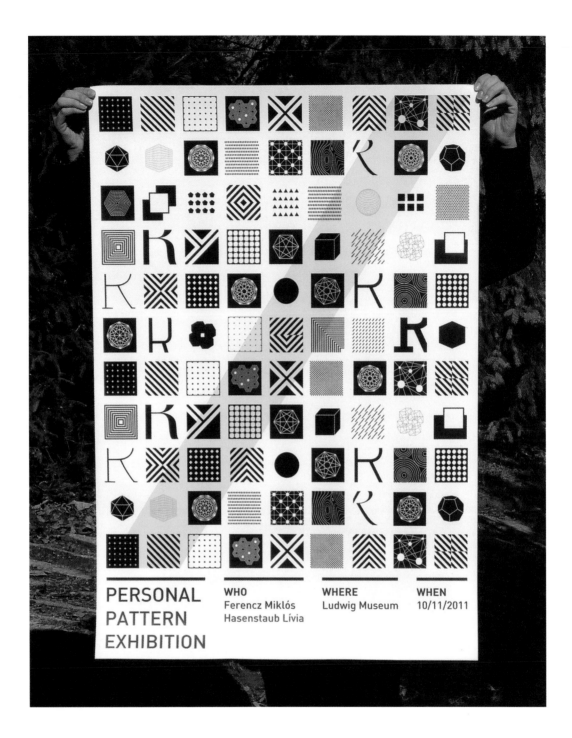

Personal Pattern

Poster manifesting a graphic summary of all creative attitudes in nine sets of typefaces and patterns in different styles. The project was initiated as a game to identify individuals' creative system as they respond and put the pieces into place.

Miklós Ferencz, Lívia Hasenstaub

Nachtschicht #4

Flyer announcing a party at the St. Gallen Art
Museum. The grey colours explored visions
in the dark.

Larissa Kasper, Rosario Florio
Client: Kunstverein St. Gallen

Tobi30

Party invitation to celebrate the 30th birthday of the designer's friend. A blank box was reserved to address the guests.

Larissa Kasper, Rosario Florio
Client: Tobias Siebrecht

Michel Meier Identity

Business cards introducing photography collective,
Jean-Marie Michel and Fanny Meier, as new a character called Michel Meier. A die-cut focus sign, standard
instant film size and black and white worked as a
visual cue for the duo's profession.

A3 Collectif

Client/ Photo: Michel Meier Photographe

"Here, black
and white is an
evidence because
that was how
photography
began."

Pins & Threads

Experimental typographic treatment using materials to communicate context in poster art and CD sleeves. This one presents thread and pins.

Kasper Pyndt Studio

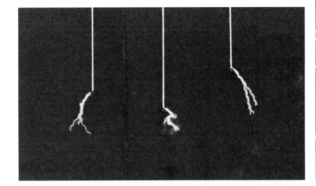

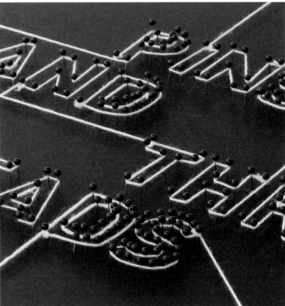

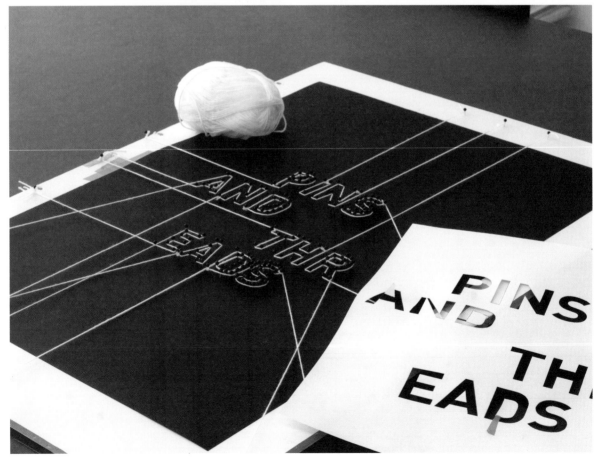

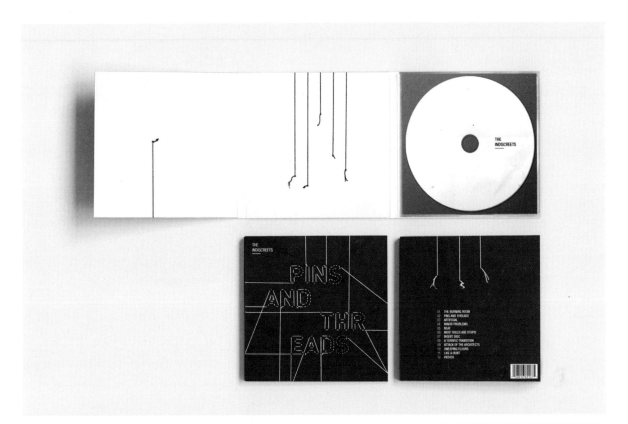

Vinyl Cover
with Analog Light
Animation

Vinyl record design for composer Allan
Gravgaard Madsen. As the disc spins, the
side with *Waves* (2009) displays undulating
waves of dots. The other side with *Crystal
Tapastry* (2010) plays rolling crystals in opposite directions in circular tracks.

Michael Hansen
Client: Allan Gravgaard Madsen

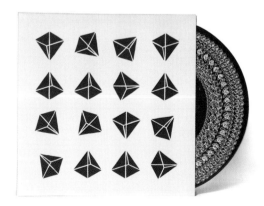

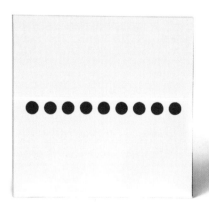

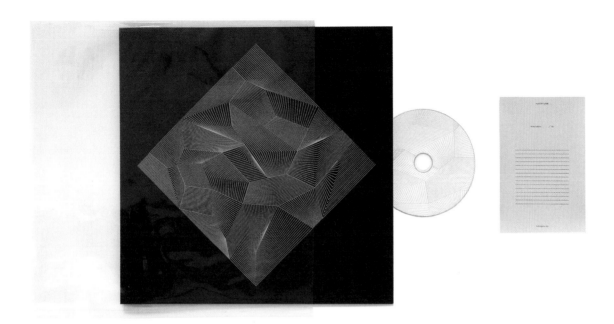

Hunter Game

Disc sleeve ornamented with arithmetically-structured pattern that extends to the disc with thin grey lines on cyber white. The numbering style for limited art projects repeats on the sleeve's back and complimentary note.

ARTIVA DESIGN
Client: Hunter Game

Designers Talk Session

Posters for Designers Talk Session at Sapporo Design Week 2009. Thanks to the thin paper, dark solid stripes on opposite sides interchanged and lent a new perspective to the design in light, like the participants did at the event.

COMMUNE

Client: Japanese Society of Commercial Space Designers (Hokkaido brunch)

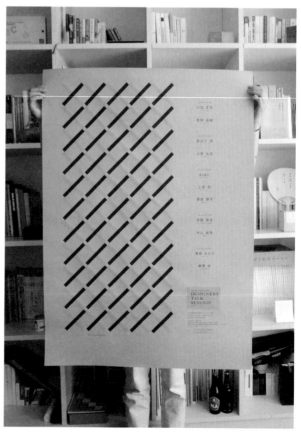

Paper Fortress

Branding and corporate stationery for independent
film production studio, Paper Fortress. The handwrit-
ings were sought to balance the owner's youthful at-
titude with his refined, professional work ethic to befit
any genre of film he involves.

Hovercraft Studio

Client: Paper Fortress

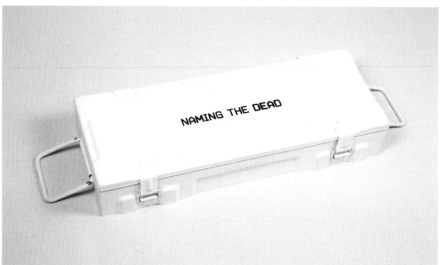

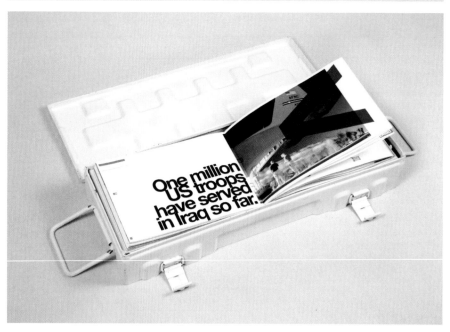

NAMING THE DEAD

Editorial and packaging design for a book that
narrated the stories of 176 British soldiers
who sacrified in the war with Iraq.

Bravo&Tango

Semperoper

Booklets published for premières held at Semperoper, a historical opera house and concert hall in
Dresden, Germany.

Fons Hickmann m23
(Susann Stefanizen, Björn Wolf, Fons Hickmann)
Client: Semper Opera Dresden

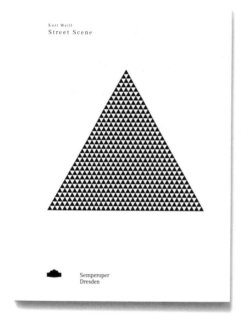

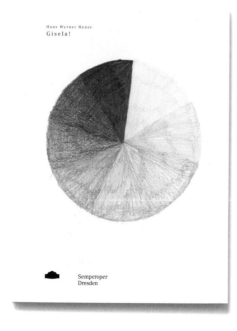

Antonín Dvořák
Rusalka

Semperoper
Dresden

Gaetano Donizetti
L'elisir d'amore

Semperoper
Dresden

Wolfgang Amadeus Mozart
Le nozze di Figaro

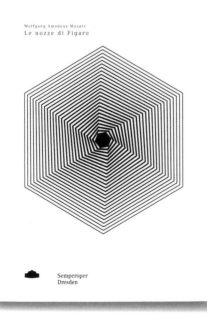

Semperoper
Dresden

Richard Strauss
Elektra

Semperoper
Dresden

Pietro Lingeri architetto della Tramezzina

Exhibition brochure and posters for exhibition, The Island of Artist, introducing Pietro Lingeri's architecture in Tremezzo, a classic of rationalism in building design. The cover image underlined the connection between inside and outside prominent in Lingeri's design.

ARTIVA DESIGN
Client: Plug_in

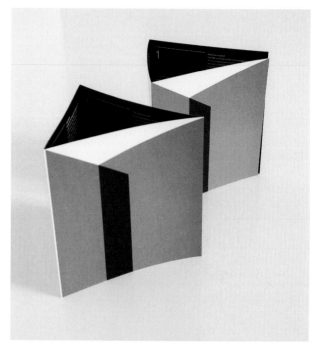

PLACE

Visual identity and collateral for PLACE, a night club for electronic music events. Shapes and dark, cold colours were used to erect a taste of "underground".

Tadas Karpavičius
Client: PROMOPHOBIA

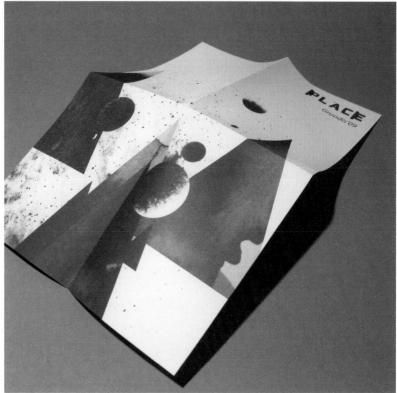

42 Architects

Flexible identity system covering branding and stationery design for architectural
design house, 42 Architects. Handstamps
were made to let 42's name stand out in
its clearest and brightest form on any
medium to hand.

Johanna Bonnevier
Client: 42 Architects

42

Teaser Campaign SS '11

A lighthearted way to introduce Just B.'s new
fashion collection and distribution points.
The facts and messages were imparted as
several news articles about Just B. spotted by
a friend who then mailed out the clippings
with personal remarks.

Smel

Client: Just B.

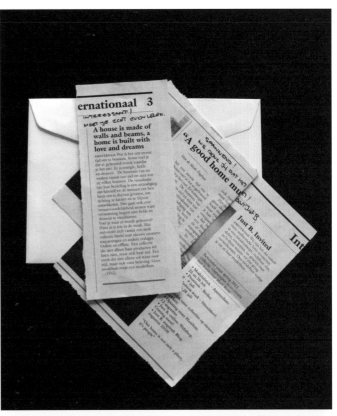

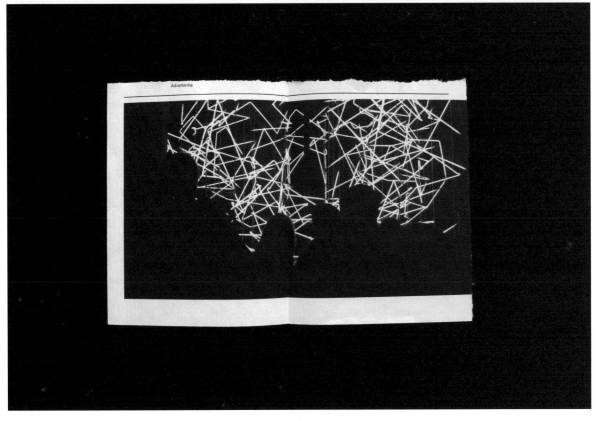

300

Poster for collective exhibition, VA300-
Con/Temporary Exhibition. Artwork
portrayed '300' as a celebration for the
school's 300th birthday.

C100 Purple Haze

Client: University of Applied Sciences
Augsburg

Nike Just Do It

Graphic explorations on Nike's Just Do It motto
using only black spots on white.

Mark Brooks Graphik Design
Client: Nike USA

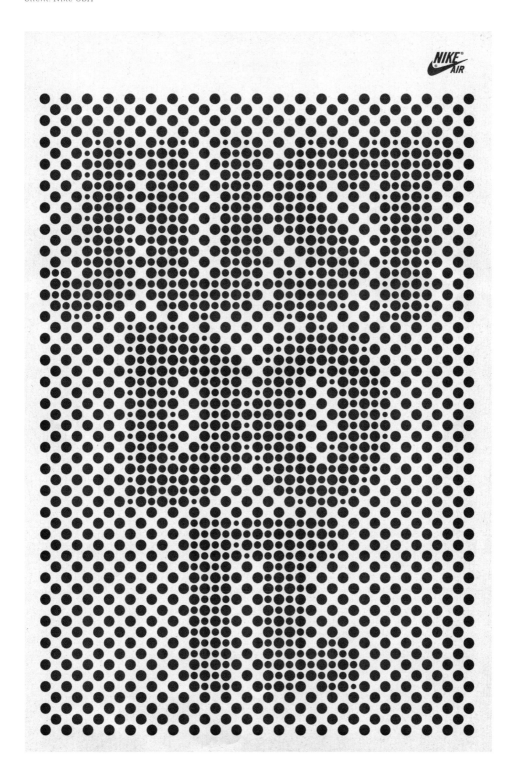

5 Years

Posters commemorating the fifth anniversary of designer's twin brother's death in an accident. While '5' marked the years of their separation, the cross laid the steps to heaven.

Joan Ramon Pastor

Model: Estela Díaz

5 AÑOS

"It's about my twin brother's death so black and white was the best combination to transmit how I felt."

DESCRYPTOR

21.08.2010   9 40

Deutschland   Deutschland   1   Sozialdemokratisch   **A23**   **R,I**

Tach! Julius

Ruhrpottsprache: *Abgezappt, anpown, fickbel, bedröppelt, sich balimmeln, bec lötwaken, fuuschkran, füffkin, küllefin, Kllaov, kniffte, meschugge, pichalo, Püllken, Schmacken.*

Technik- und Ingenieurs-   Diplom
wissenschaften

Allein   3 (3)   5

DESCRYPTOR

Großbritannien

Mahlzeit!

Hamburgerisch: *Allbacktnack, onkooken, hanghüx, Untermunnlode, kartendüller klei mi an de Fent, kloik twee, Noktel, nülflooten, tadelg, zuppendufter.*

Abitur

Partnerlich   0 (1)   2

Descryptor

Eumann's diploma-thesis on developing an interactive system to analyse and render data of individuals into highly personalised posters. Precision and objectivity were underlined using mono-colours, among varying line-weights to create shades of grey.

Jan Eumann

*Special credits: Prof. Reinhard, Prof. Malsy,
Mortimer Neuss, Stefan Rüschenberg*

21.06.2010   9:57

3   Ungpolitisch | C12 | E |

Melanie

DESCRYPTOR

21.08.2010   9:17

Deutschland   Deutschland   2   Liberal | C2 | A,S |

Hi!   Jan

Ruhrpottsprache: *Abgezoppt, anpesen, Babbel, bedröppelt, sich heimmeln, boe, Dönekes, flutschkato, küffen, Killefitt, Klüsen, Knifte, meschugge, picheln, Pölleken, Schnucken.*

Radiohead —«Street Spirit»
Trentemøller —«Pull the Beginning of the End»
The Knife —«Colouring of Pigeons»

Kunst und Design   Diplom

Wohngemeinschaft   0 (2)   2

Ausdauersport

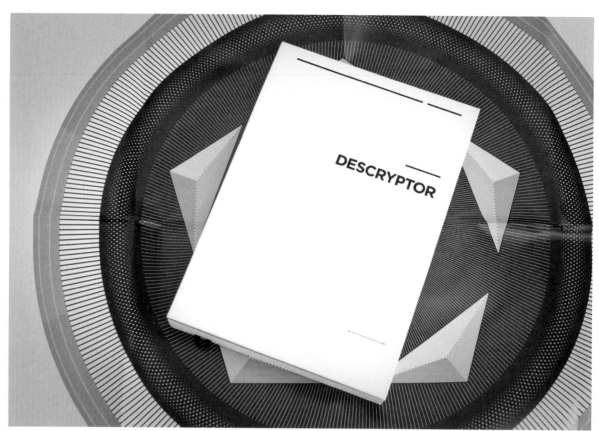

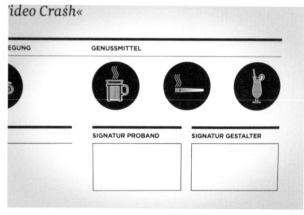

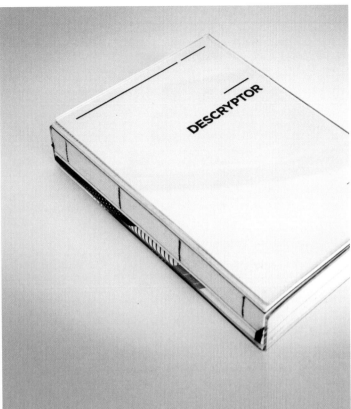

YOUR NEW FLAGSHIP OPENING 18 MARCH

TOPSHOP
Sergelgatan

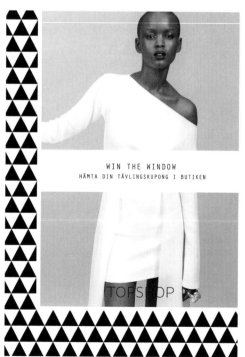

WIN THE WINDOW
HÄMTA DIN TÄVLINGSKUPONG I BUTIKEN

TOPSHOP

FREDAG 18 MARS — SÖNDAG 27 MARS

Styla din egen look i Topshops godbitar och posera
sen i vårt fotobås och ta med ett minne hem från din
upplevelse i den nya Topshop-butiken på Sergelgatan.
Kolla in vårt galleri och tagga dig själv på
www.facebook.com/topshopsverige

TOPSHOP

Topshop Sergelgatan

Branding, press and marketing materials for
Topshop's new branch opening in Stockholm. The
triangular pattern referenced the iconic design of
Sergeis Torg's public square nearby and inspired
other elements, such as typeface and colour
scheme.

Johanna Bonnevier

Client: Topshop

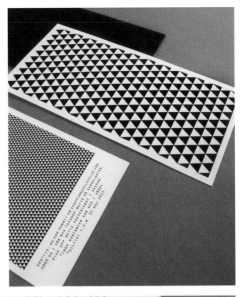

Haute Couture Busts

Patterned mannequins elevated from pure lay figures to arresting high-fashion pieces with significant artistic merit. Stockman, who collaborated in manufacturing the models, was a well-respected bustform maker based in France.

Emmanuel Bossuet, Stockman

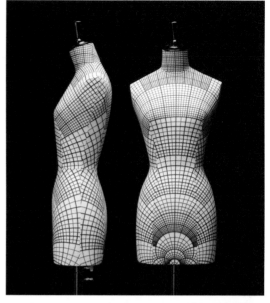

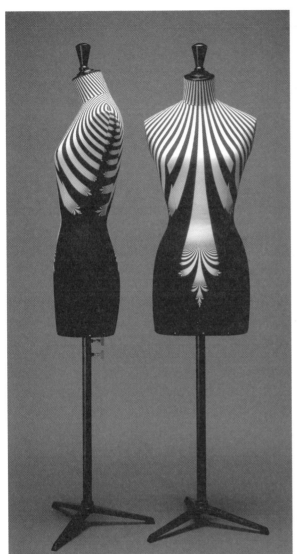

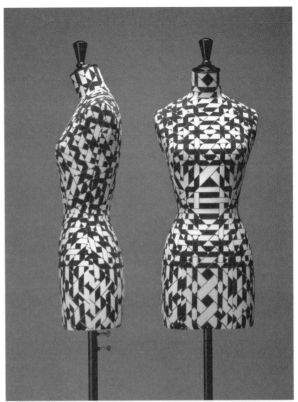

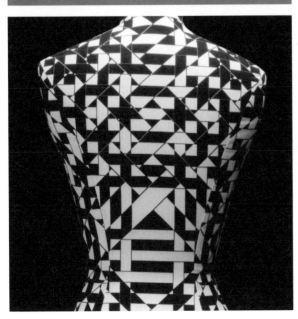

Winter Collections

Fine digital prints on silk scarves revolving around designer's own peculiar visual universe and encounter with her fields of interest, such as collage works and animal totems. These mufflers come in an array of shapes and sizes with luxury finish by hand.

Coco

Photo: Gilles Danger
Client: Forget-Me-Not

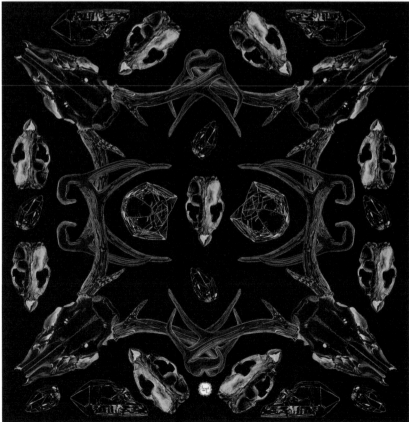

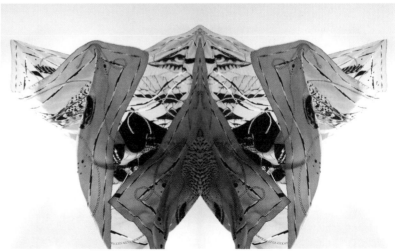

Armley Mills

New identity for Armley Mills, formerly the world's largest woollen mill commercially operated between 1808 and 1969. The line graphics reserved its illustrious history and celebrated the process of wool manufacture from start to end.

John Barton
Client: Armley Mills

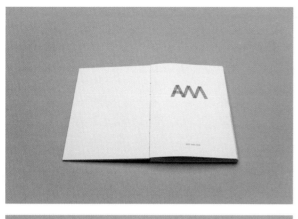
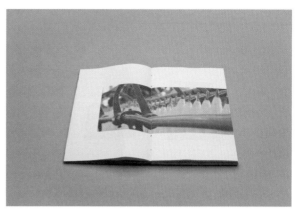
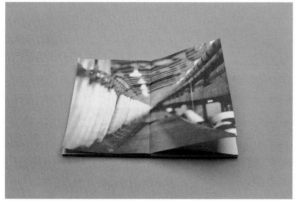
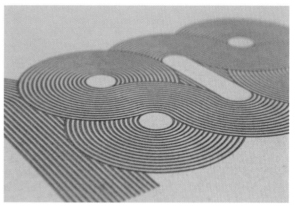

Edited BLACK Comme des Garçons X Asylum

Limited tote bags and pin badges that mark the first collaboration between BLACK CDG and Asylum. Inspired by children's innocence, the graphic scheme revolved around the tenet of Black Bird Singing, Black Star Shining and Black Tree Growing with an offbeat sense of optimism resonant of BLACK CDG's spirit.

Asylum

Photo: Lumina Photography

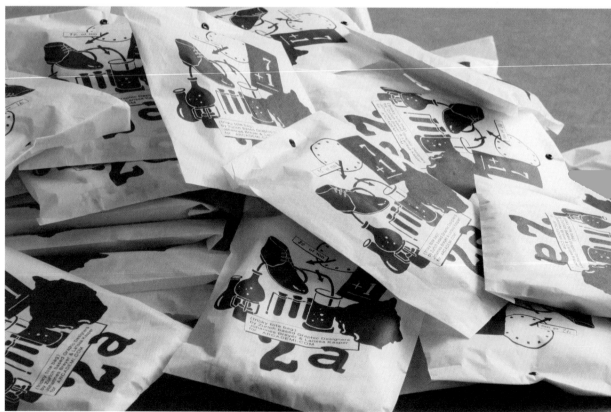

ARCADEMI Affaires

Cotton bags for the second edition of ARCADEMI
Affaires, featuring a silkscreened image-puzzle-
riddle to be solved. The bags came with a paper
bag with an edition of 100.

Larissa Kasper, Rosario Florio
Client: Moritz Firchow, ARCADEMI

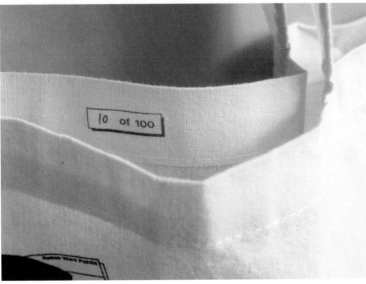

FRAKTUR   EINS   1/100

Editions of 100

Original limited edition poster prints published with
an edition of 100. Featured here, from left to right, are
Fraktur and *Brévent* by BERG, and *Kompakt-kassette* by
Daniel Freytag. BERG's prints tend to explore texture
and express depth in black and white.

BERG

"Infographics without colours are sexy."

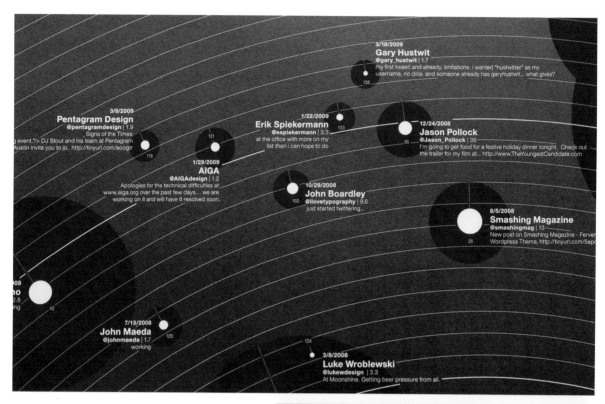

Cosmic 140

Web Trend Map charting facts about the world's most influential Twitterers from different area of interest. Data included their joining year, first tweet, frequency of tweets per day and the number of followers they have.

Information Architects

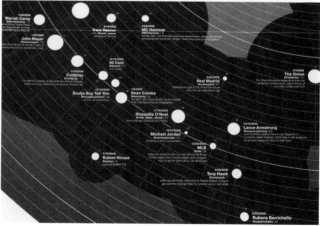

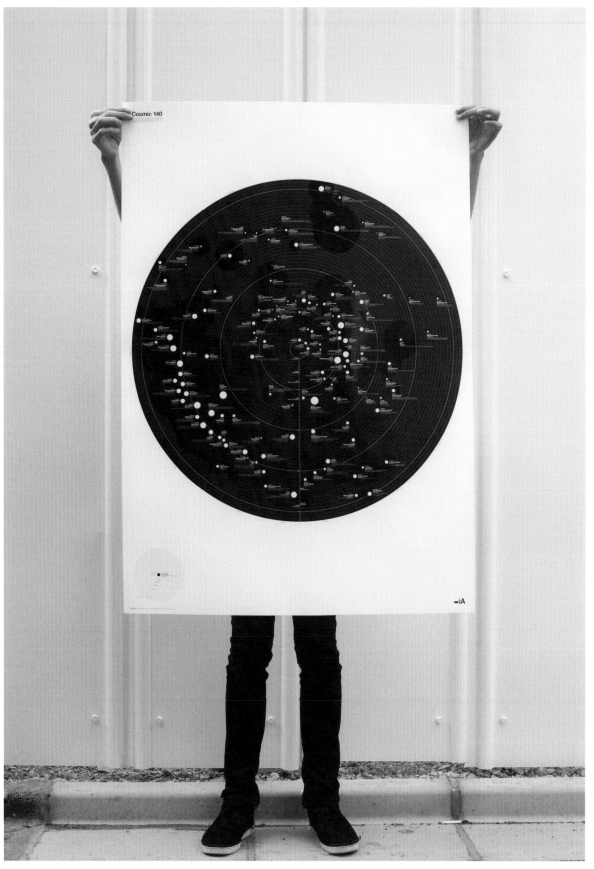

Schwarmverhalten

Three booklets playing on format to point at a designer's thoughts, problems and attitudes while working on a book, from the perspectives of two designers. The result was a blend of *Liner Notes* (2009)'s literary content and Bertholt Brechts' epic theatre theories.

Larissa Kasper, Rosario Florio

Typography: Johannes Breyer
Mentor: Kurt Eckert (Zurich University of the Art)

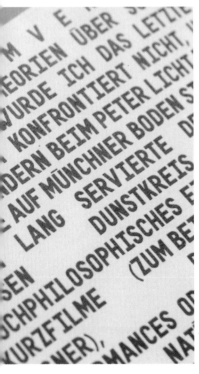

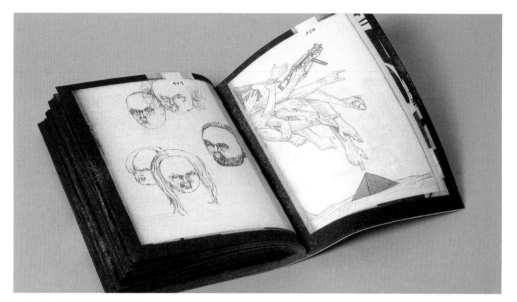

Gessnerallee Illustrations

A book of striking programme images by young Swiss graphic artists, compiled to mark the end of a seven-year collaboration between Raffinerie and Gessnerallee theatre in Zurich. It is a tactile take too, on the motivations behind the project.

Raffinerie AG für Gestaltung

The Geometry of Pasta

The Geometry of Pasta points up pasta shapes and matching sauce as the key to perfect a dish. Graphically outlined, the pastas on the cover gave readers a taste of the book's unique and witty approach to cooking alongside recipes by chef Jacob Kenedy.

Here Design
Client: Boxtree, Macmillan Publishers

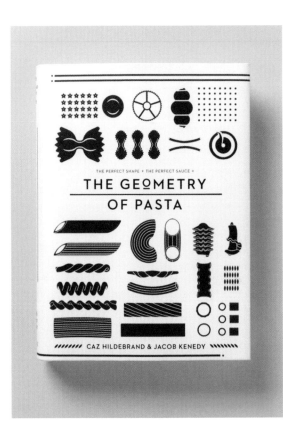

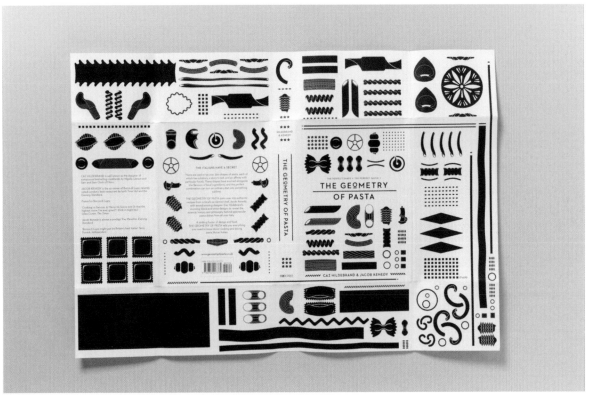

ROBERT GELLER AW10
Show Invitation

A/W '10 fashion show invitation for New York-based men's
fashion brand, ROBERT GELLER, using ink on newsprint.
The frames in inverted colours on opposite sides converted
RG's iconic logo to denote the blessing year 2010.

STUDIO NEWWORK

Client: ROBERT GELLER

Foreign Rights
Frankfurt 2010
Non Fiction Books

Grupo Planeta

Foreign
Rights
Frankfurt 2010
Children

Grupo Planeta [GRUP 62]

Foreign Rights
Frankfurt 2010
Grup 62

[GRUP 62]

Foreign
Rights
Frankfurt 2010
Fiction Books

Grupo Planeta

Foreign Rights Catalogues

Catalogue design based on quotation marks to indicate authors'
rights. The different type styles characterise four book categories:
Fiction, Non-Fiction, Children literature and *Grup 62.*

Studio Astrid Stavro

Client: Planeta

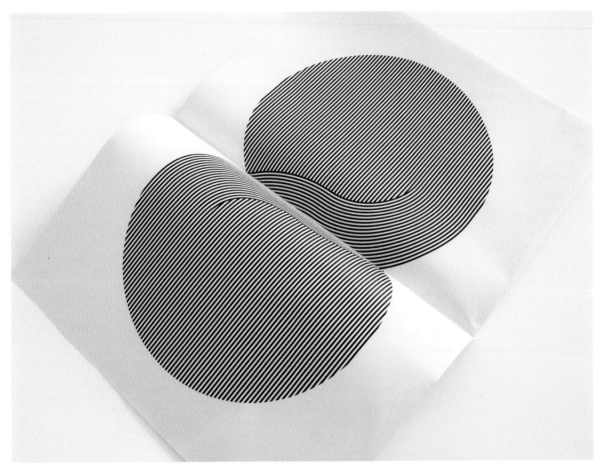

A.D. Nothing to Read

A journal-poster made to incentivise viewers to reflect upon the meaning of communication in the absence of words. It is a question with no answers. Viewers can interpret from whichever angles and however they like.

ARTIVA DESIGN

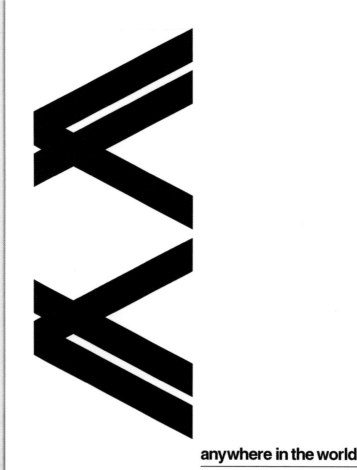

anywhere in the world

anywhere in the world is the promotional poster of rui ribeiro.
He is trying to get a placement anywhere in the world as he is applying to a grant that will
allow him to be that ambitious.

Created on purpose for the iNOV-ART program.
Promotional piece by Rui Ribeiro.
© 2011 www.cofseeing.com

"I perceive it as an all-or-nothing, straightforward message. It allows for a more thorough process of thinking when it comes to information priority."

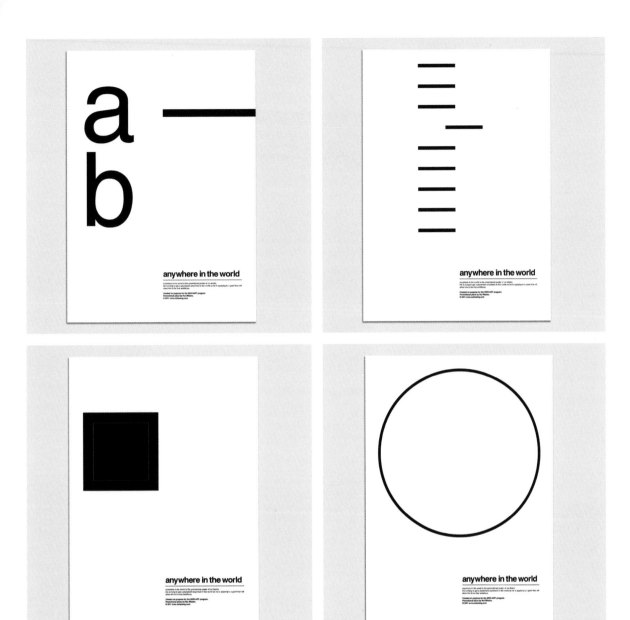

Anywhere in the World.

Ribeiro was thinking he could go "anywhere in the world" for a placement. Six graphic posters expressing his notion and vision of world, travelling or specialty were composed as a promotional project to introduce himself.

Rui Ribeiro

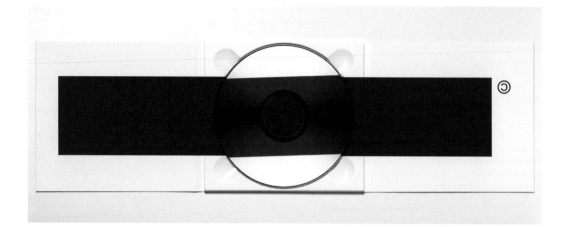

Anonymous

Identity for Anonymous which opposes Internet censorship and watch. The logo, as good as a censor bar, implies information blackout with an anti-authoritative voice. Black and white is authentically Anonymous' spirit and visually strengthens the logo design.

Mads Jakob Poulsen

Back up your files —*we are coming to visit.*

Sincerely

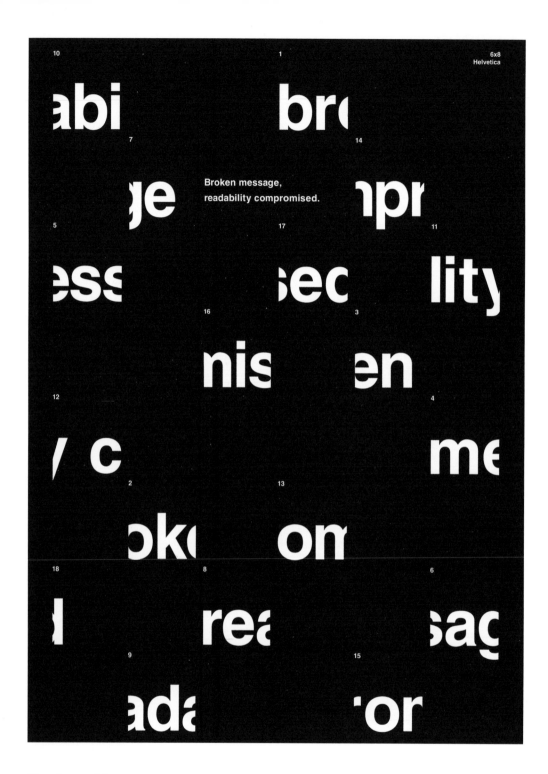

Broken message,
readability compromised.

Broken Message,
Readability Compromised.

A project approaching the literal idea of a broken message by imagining the possible impact and chaos that an untreated message can cause.

Rui Ribeiro

Abbruchhaus

Announcement for a party to happen in a club in Zurich. To reso-
nate with the event's giveaway – a lasercut fabric diamond by Jakob
Schläpfer. Qualities of light refractions were injected into the type
design, printed on 45gsm white paper with metallic coating.

Larissa Kasper, Rosario Florio
Client: Abbruchhaus.net

"Black and white make the artwork simple and direct in its message."

Looking for Magic

Whimsical landscapes composed of outlandish flora and fauna with elements of infographics. Prints were developed exclusively for Anywalk footwear's touring exhibiton 'Trekx'.

Emily Forgot
Client: Anywalk

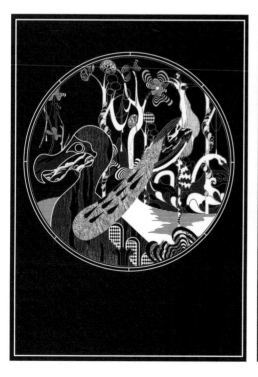

Anna Mun Olla

Identity for "Anna mun olla (Let Me Be)", showcasing art pieces about and created by disabled people. The collateral completed the theme with the exhibition's highlights.

Lotta Nieminen, Mikko Luotonen

Client: Annantalo Culture Center (Helsinki, Finland)

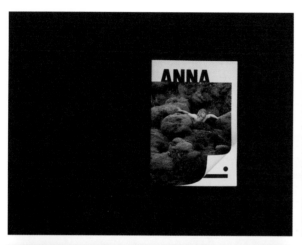

We Love Geometry

Modular grid, shapes and lines —
geometry exists in diverse forms.
Introduced as abstracted numbers,
the structural digits on both sides of
these posters progress into distinct
structural patterns as they unfold.

Ibán Ramón + Dídac Ballester

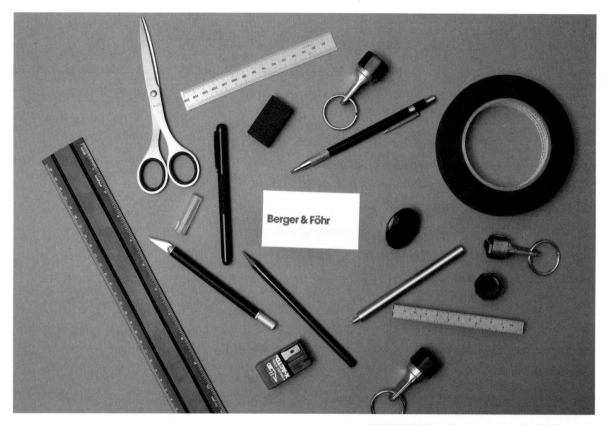

Berger & Föhr Studio Collateral

Berger & Föhr's belief for lasting visual communication solutions is built in their constant search for modernistic expressions and objectivity. The same applied to their own collateral with uniform type size, grids and a neutral colour scheme, based on the "rule of thirds".

Berger & Föhr Studio
Letterpress: Sweet Letter Press
Photo: Jamie Kripke

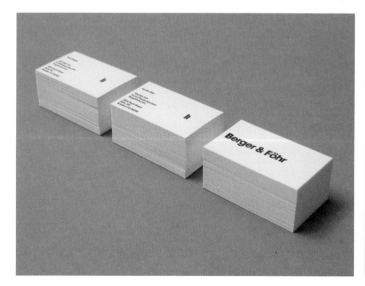

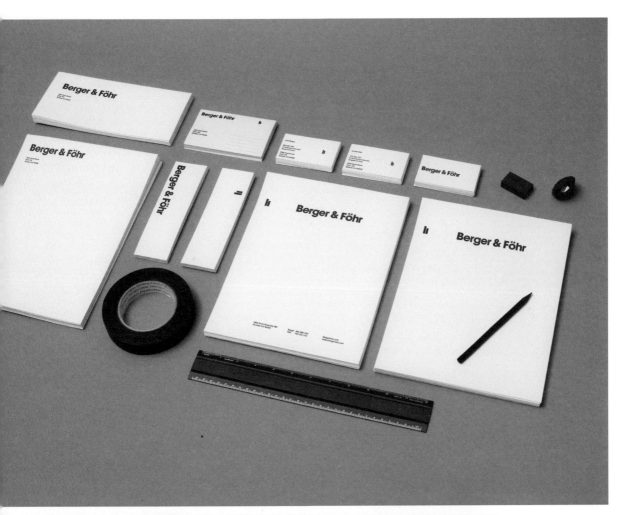

The Necessity
of Silence

Packaging and poster for a book of interviews
with world-famous composers on writing
music for cinema. The 12 alphabets in distinctive fonts denote the 12 interviewees by their
initials, with black or white space indicative of
'silence' as a basic sound element itself.

Edited

Author: Angela Law
Client: kubrick (Hong Kong)

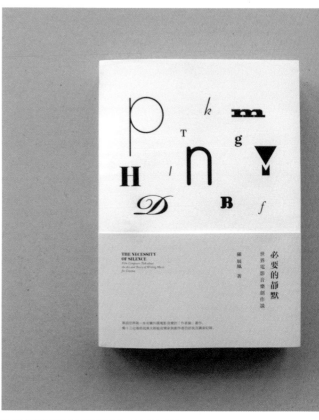

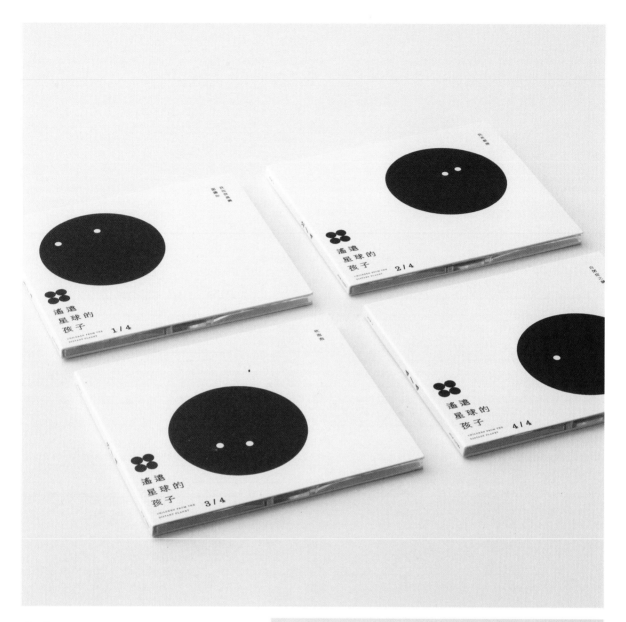

Children from the Distant Planet

Simple yet expressive, the four mouth-less faces illustrated a muted and isolated world in where autistic children live. Started off as a low-budget solution, the documentary box set packaging gives an illustrative and solemn introduction to the mental disorder.

Wang Zhi Hong

Client: Atom Cinema

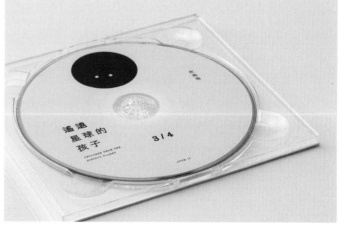

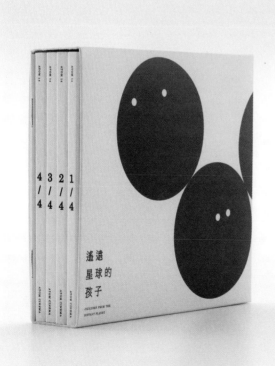

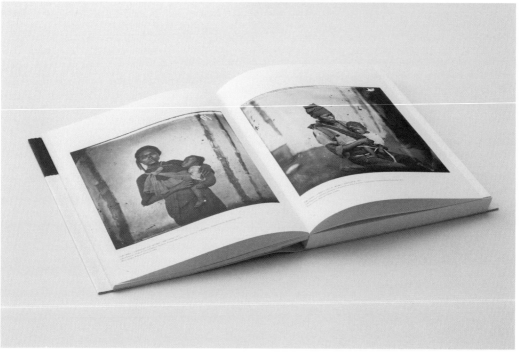

"Visually, words are at their best in black or white."

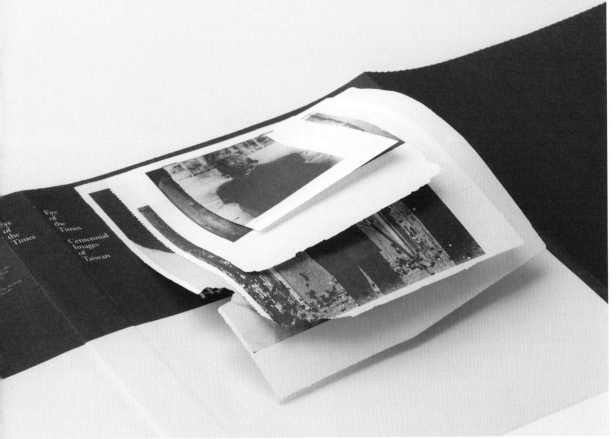

Eye of the Times

Packaging for the chronicle of Taiwan's 100 years of development, to publish along an exhibition of its namesake. Selective pictures were reproduced with artificially tattered edges as a visual punch for the history book.

Wang Zhi Hong

Client: Taipei Fine Art Museum

The Heart is a Lonely Hunter

Cover design for the Chinese edition of Carson McCullers' *The Heart Is a Lonely Hunter* (1940). The fragmented title visualised a scene in the novel about light and shadow, with a sense of lonely silence in its warm, grey space.

Wang Zhi Hong
Client: Freedom Hill

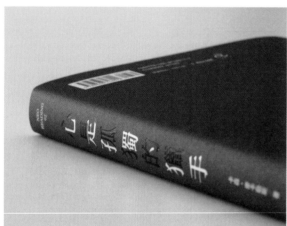

We work in cooperation
with professionals from many
business fields in order to make
their excellence possible and visible.

Identity.
Strategy.
Communication.

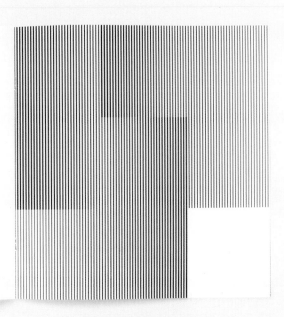

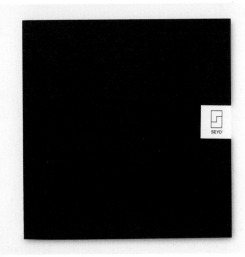

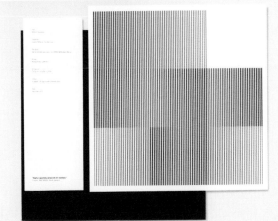

SEYO Brochure

Brochure and silkscreens for SEYO,
a medical business advisor. The
overlapping patterns allude to SEYO's
dedication to pursuing excellence
with its customers side by side.

ARTIVA DESIGN
Client: SEYO

Lezioni di paesaggio 2#

Flyers and posters for Lezioni di paesaggio,
where architects, artists and geographers
met to promote environmental awareness.
The elements presented the dualities of the
event, where opposing views converged.

ARTIVA DESIGN

Client: Plug_in edition

lezioni di paesaggio #2
sperimentazioni tra
arte e architettura

1 - 4 luglio 2009
colonia di renesso
savignone - ge

workshop:
Stefano Boccalini, artista
Mario Galvagni, architetto

organizzazione e cura:
Emanuele Piccardo
in collaborazione con Archphoto.it

iscrizioni e informazioni entro il 20/6/2009
info@plugin-lab.it
tel+fax: 010 9643822

plug_in

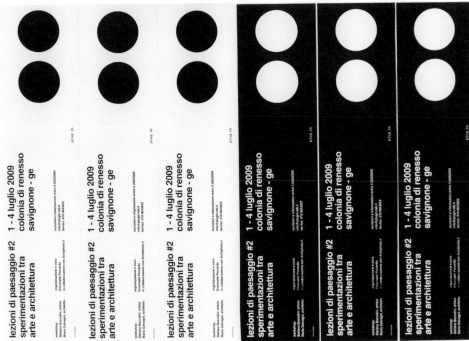

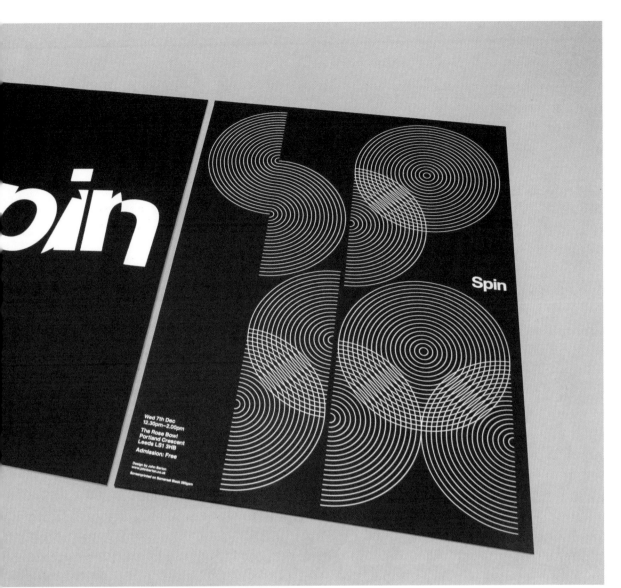

Wed 7th Dec
12.30pm–2.00pm
The Rose Bowl
Portland Crescent
Leeds LS1 3HB
Admission: Free

Design by John Barton
www.johnbarton.co.uk

Screenprinted on Somerset Black 250gsm

Spin

Spin

Spinx2

Two guests, two posters. The double-sided
posters introduced the guest lecturers from
Spin as part of VLP in Leeds. The studio's
name was interpreted by its literal sense, with
a feeling of movement.

John Barton
Client: Visiting Lecture Programme (VLP)

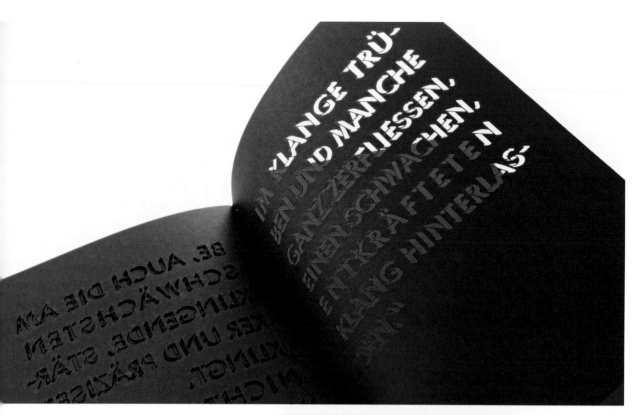

Ästhetik Jenseits des Sichtbaren

Titled *Aesthetics Beyond The Visible*, the three books were produced as an attempt to conceive messages with multiple techniques but offsetting and colour contrasts. Colour theories of Wassily Kandinsky and Herman Melville were embodied in the execution.

Marie-Niamh Dowling

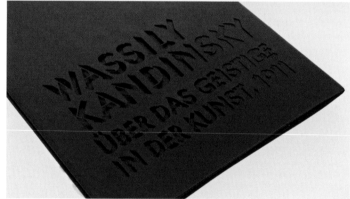

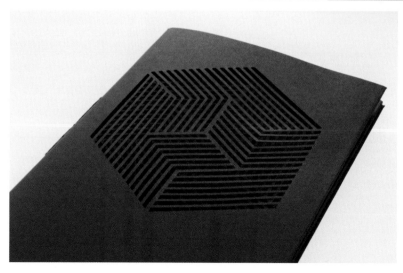

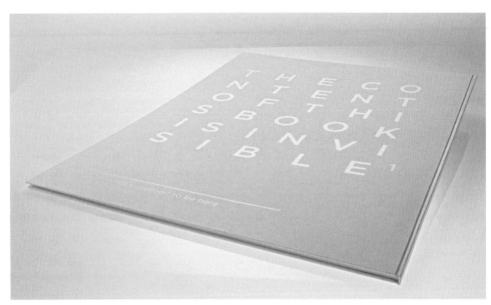

"Black and white enable other things to become visible and at the same time reduce them to their essential."

Portraits

Graphite portraits on wall. Through
true-to-life lonesome characters drawn
on blank surfaces and interactions with
space and lighting on site, Del Valle's
works are part fiction, part memory,
focusing on forms and matters.

Cesar Del Valle

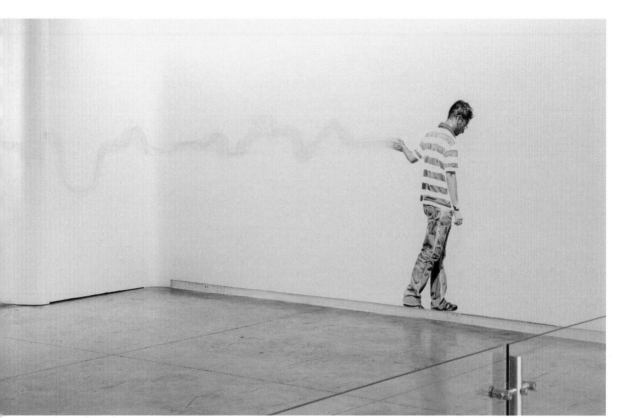

Memories in
Black and White

Two compact blocks of boxes and
everyday objects construed as 'memories' in volume and distinctive colours,
exhibited at Zona Maco, Mexico City in
April, 2012.

Michael Johansson

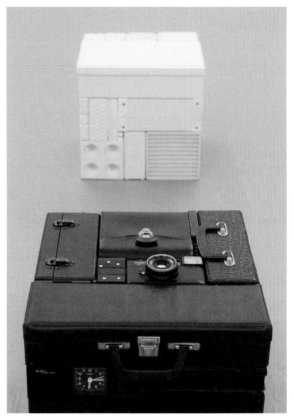

NITS DE MACBA

Print and digital flyers to announce the start of night-time sessions at MACBA. The audience was precisely pictured as "night owls", penetrating gaze into the dark and eagerly awaiting the MACBA nights.

ruiz+company

Client: MACBA: Museum of Contemporary Art Barcelona

NITS DE MACBA

**DEL 25/06 AL 23/09
DIJOUS I DIVENDRES
DE 20 A 24h**

VISITES GUIADES INCLOSES

MUSEU
D'ART CONTEMPORANI
DE BARCELONA

www.macba.cat

Patrocinador de comunicació

el Periódico

Amb el suport de:

SCANNERFM

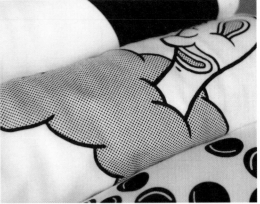

Diners T-shirts

Five limited edition T-shirt pack designs for members of Erste Bank's Diners Club. Each tee is presented in a carton envelope, both with a graphic interpretation of a capital 'D' for 'Diners Club'.

Bunch

Illustration: Dora Budor & Maja Čule, OKO, Krekhaus, Pekmezmed, Tena Letica
Client: Erste Card Club d.d.

Greyscale Collection

A collection of commissions and
studio projects taking on tones of grey,
structure and typefaces to excite.

This Studio

Photo: Andrew Penketh

1-3. Launch Posters / Client: Alan Cook
4. Electro / Client: Nitzen, Edits by Edit
5,6. Homage Hofmann / Client: This Studio
7,8. Launch Posters – Giles and Jill /
Client: Neil Gavin Photography
9. This Year / Client: This Studio

1

2

3

elecTr0

4

5

6

7

8

9

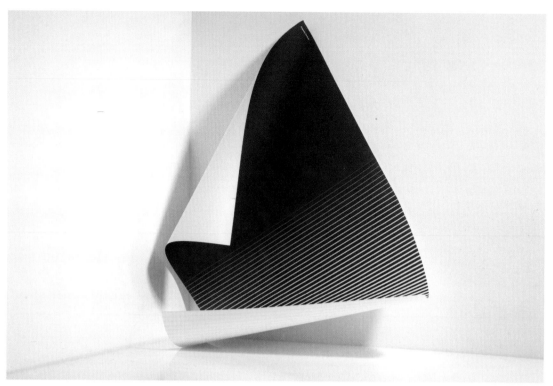

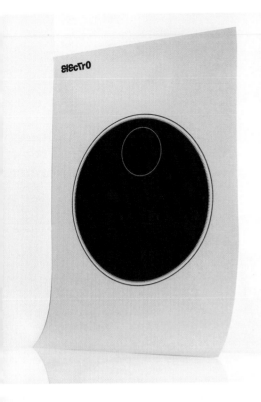

"Black and white help me concentrate on the form and structure of what I am designing. It's the simplest to reproduce and for me has the most impact."

Thermo

Murmure's first thermo-sensitive
business cards and posters play
magic, displaying alternative results
at every touch. Although ephmeral,
they dare beholders to be creative
for wow effects.

Murmure

Murmure Identity

Murmure's in-house corporate stationery to communicate typographic elegance, sensuality and technological and conceptual innovation supported by fineness and texture of paper stock.

Murmure

"Black is often a reference to the photography world. A presence to the eye that no other colour can provide."

2012

A simple new year greeting sublimated
into the subtleties of whites and light
through graphic refinement and technical
complexity on a greeting card.

Murmure

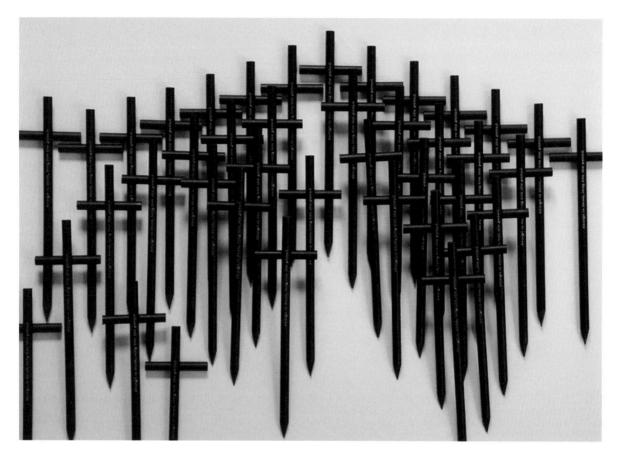

Design is Dead

An homage to pencils which have once been designers' best creative partner but gradually replaced by digital tools. The pencils were deliberately rendered as the sacred token of sacrifice with an attached "pencil rest".

STUDIOLAV

A to Z

Postcard flyer announcing a party at
club Zukunft in Zurich organised by
Abbruchhaus. The idea of demolition
implied in the organiser's name was
explored with an eroded and destruct-
ed type.

Larissa Kasper, Rosario Florio
Client: Abbruchhaus.net

Eine

New identity for British graffitist,
Ben Eine's website and stationery,
referencing the black paint drips on
the edges of the artist's canvas. Eine's
initial was embossed in his signature
typeface, Circus, as his personal mark.

Root
Client: Ben Eine

"Black and white make a perfect contrast to the vibrancy of his art especially on digital platforms."

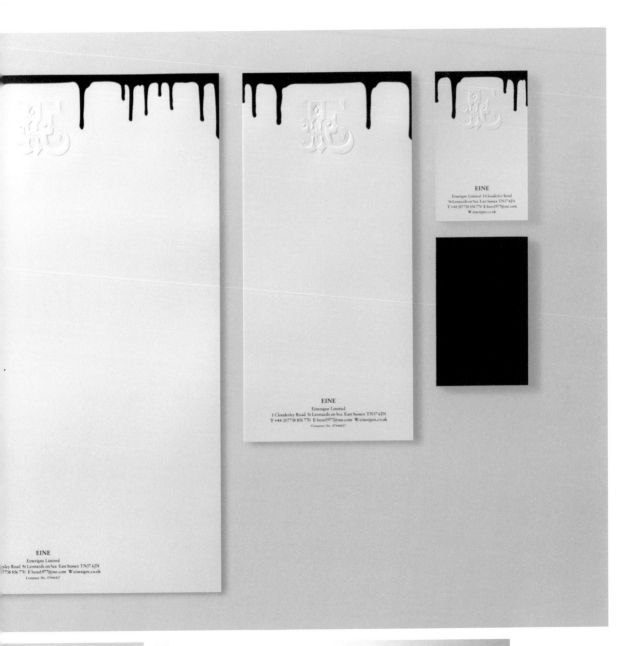

EINE
Einesigns Limited
1 Cloudesley Road St Leonards on Sea East Sussex TN37 6JN
T +44 (0)7738 856 770 E bens1977@me.com W einesigns.co.uk
Company No. 07446427

EINE
Einesigns Limited 1 Cloudesley Road
St Leonards on Sea East Sussex TN37 6JN
T +44 (0)7738 856 770 E bens1977@me.com
W einesigns.co.uk

En Haute Joaillerie

Rebranding for luxury jeweller, En Haute Joaillerie. 'En' was extracted from the name and expanded into upbeat words in a lace-like design to complement the graceful jewels and gems and visualise the attributes a gift can bring.

Asylum

Photo: Lumina Photography
Client: En Haute Joaillerie

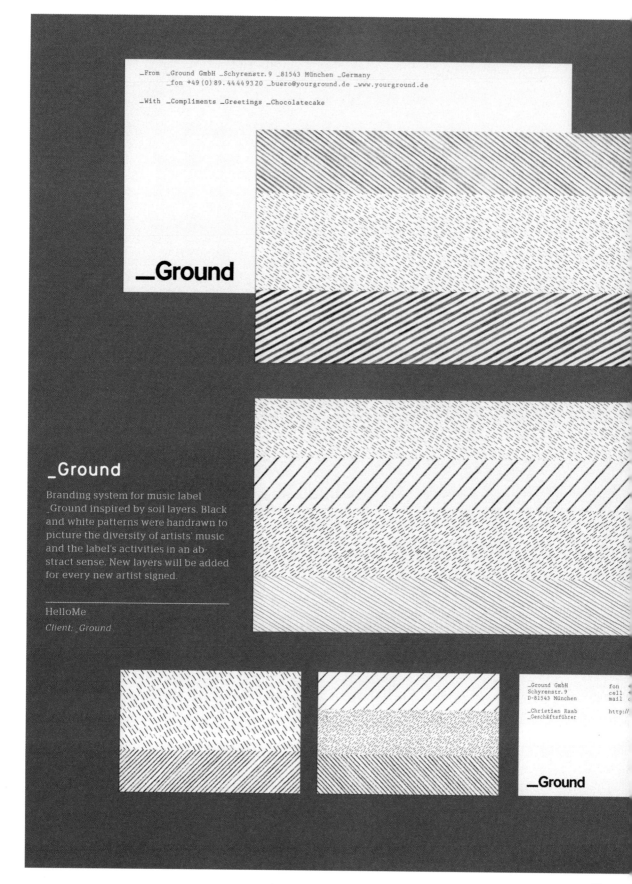

_From _Ground GmbH _Schyrenstr. 9 _81543 München _Germany
_fon +49 (0) 89. 44 44 93 20 _buero@yourground.de _www.yourground.de

_With _Compliments _Greetings _Chocolatecake

_Ground

Branding system for music label
_Ground inspired by soil layers. Black
and white patterns were handrawn to
picture the diversity of artists' music
and the label's activities in an abstract sense. New layers will be added
for every new artist signed.

HelloMe
Client: _Ground

_Ground GmbH   fon +
Schyrenstr. 9   cell +
D-81543 München   mail @

_Christian Raab   http://
_Geschäftsführer

_Ground

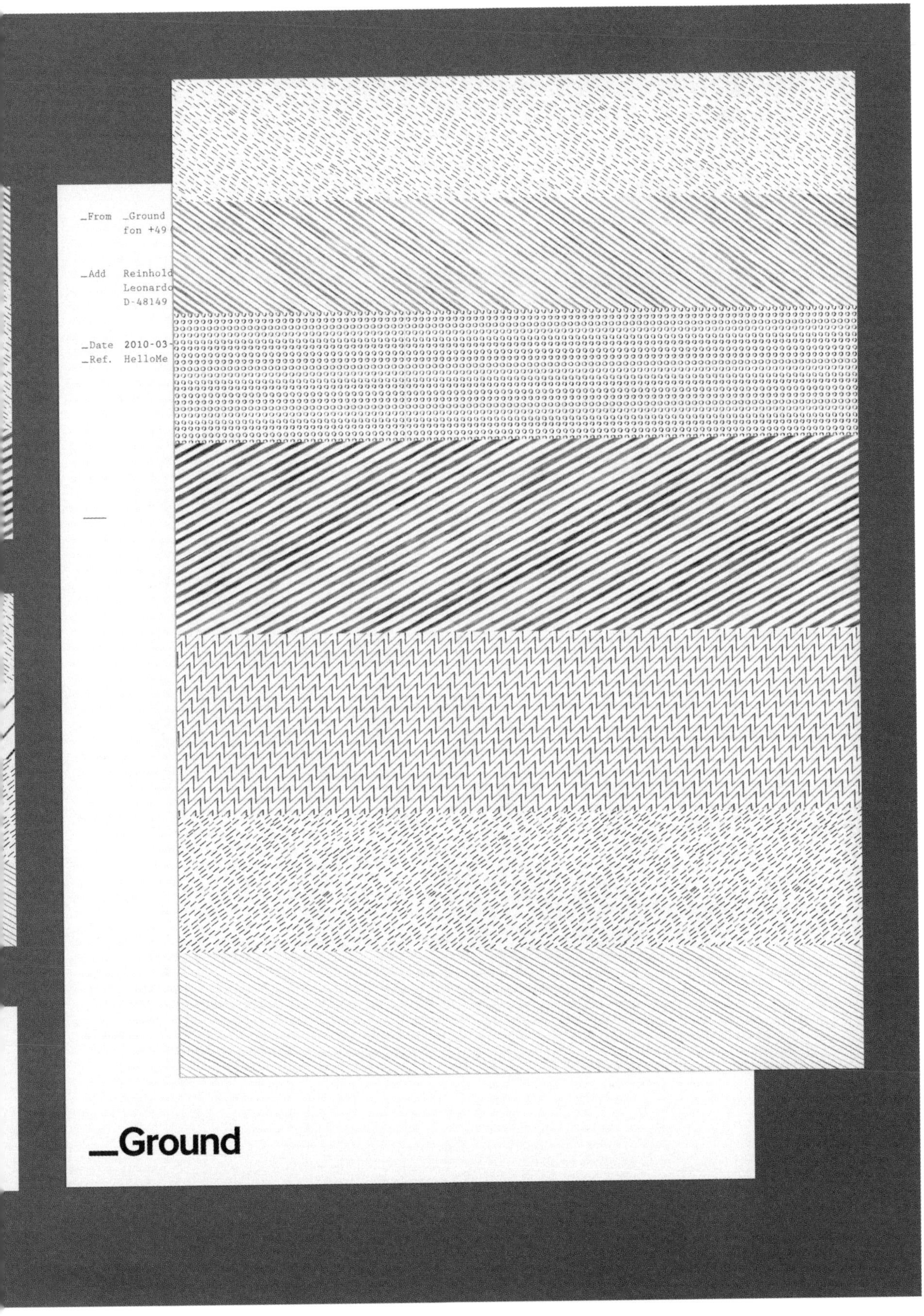

_From   _Ground
        fon +49

_Add   Reinhold
        Leonardo
        D-48149

_Date   2010-03
_Ref.   HelloMe

__Ground

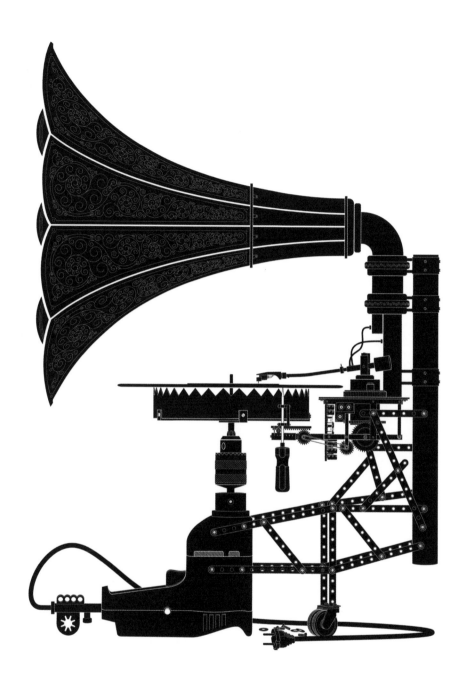

B-Sides

Posters for B-sides, an annual open-air
music festival in Lucerne, Switzerland.
While it is usually great bonus tracks on a
record's B-side, the event was visualised
as a machine trashing A-side songs, which
are often crowd-pleasers.

FEIXEN: Design by Felix Pfäffli

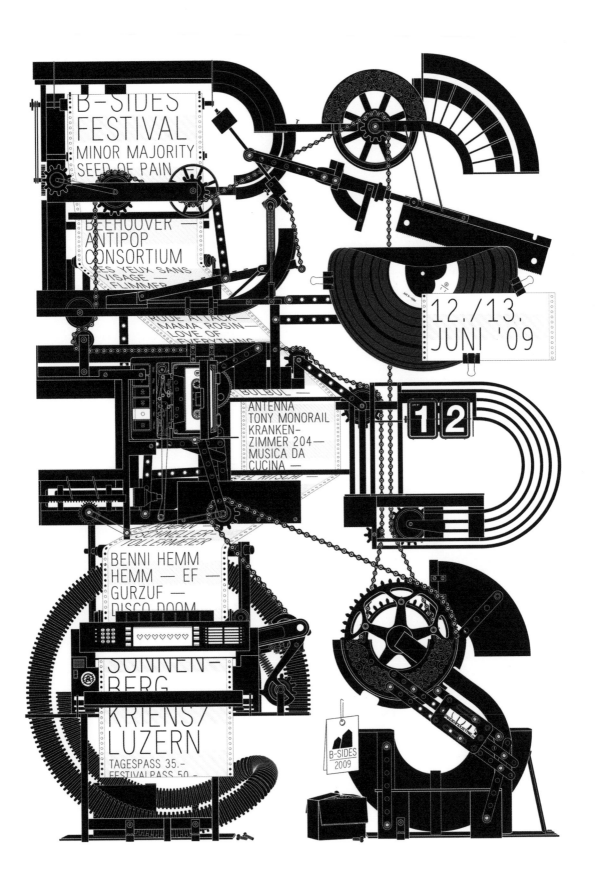

B-SIDES
FESTIVAL
MINOR MAJORITY
SEED OF PAIN

BEEHOOVER —
ANTIPOP
CONSORTIUM
LES YEUX SANS
VISAGE —
FLIMMER

RUDE ATTACK —
MAMA ROSIN —
LOVE OF
EVERYTHING

BULBUL —

ANTENNA
TONY MONORAIL
KRANKEN-
ZIMMER 204 —
MUSICA DA
CUCINA —

EL KITSCH!

HÖHER-
SCHNELLER-
TOLLERMEIER —

BENNI HEMM
HEMM — EF
GURZUF —
DISCO DOOM

SONNEN-
BERG

KRIENS/
LUZERN
TAGESPASS 35.–
FESTIVALPASS 50.–

12./13.
JUNI '09

12

B-SIDES
2009

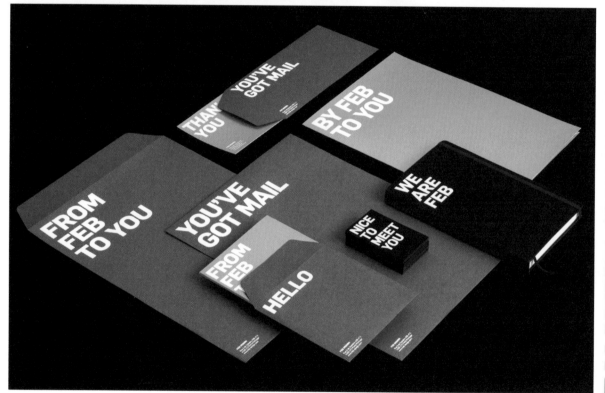

FEB Stationery

Stressing the communicative quality of individual items, media were taken as the message and central character of the stationery set. A friendly tone was adopted to reflect FEB's close relationship with customers which they nourish everyday.

FEB Design, FIBA Design

This Is Smel

A good way to know Smel is from how creative people address the team. The cheerful remarks collected from emails, notes and envelopes were converted into letterheads and taglines on business cards to introduce the dynamic and caring boys at Smel.

Smel

Bono 4 Smel

Les garçons de Smel

Bono 4 Smel

Carlo Elias
creative director

smel creative and strategic design studio
Wilgenweg 20 C / 1031 HV Amsterdam / T
T (+31.20) 486 70 50 / M (+31.6) 18 555 29
www.smel.net / c.elias@smel.net

Edgar Smaling
creative director

Fire away boys!*

Zijn we er klaar voor...?
A*

smel creative and strategic design studio
Wilgenweg 20 C / 1031 HV Amsterdam / The Netherlands

BLANC

Multiple elements for a splendid and spacious gastrobar offering all-day dining inside the Mandarin Oriental Hotel Barcelona. From the chefs' hats to its wine menus, the graphic identity scheme coheres with the restaurant's atmosphere. Communications for day and night is set apart with black and white.

Alex Dalmau

Photo: Susana Gellida
Agency: Larsson-Duprez
Client: Mandarin Oriental Barcelona

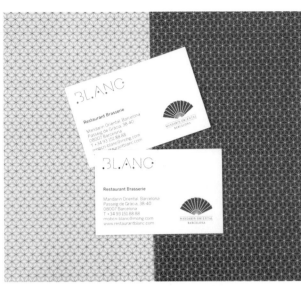

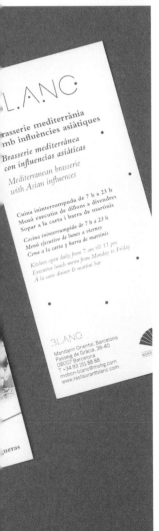

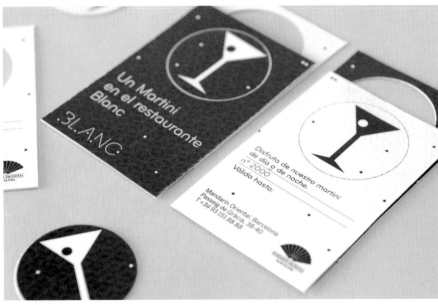

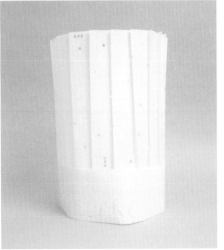

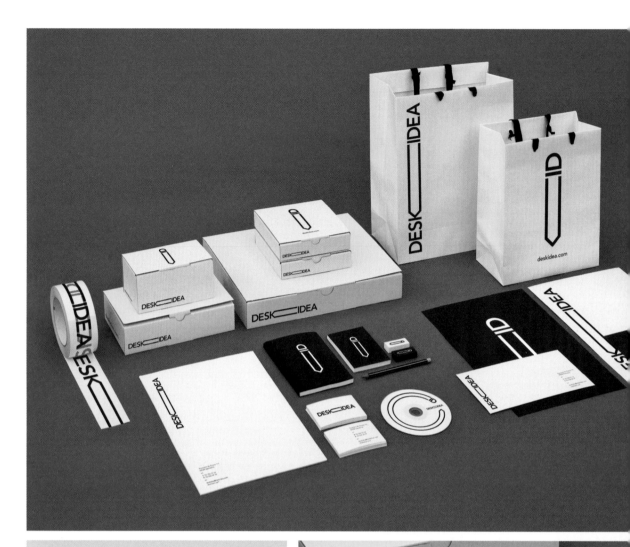

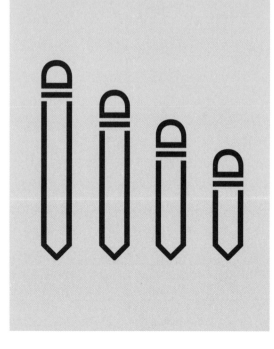

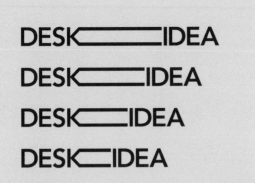

DESKIDEA

Branding for e-stationer, cleverly linking "desk" and "idea" with a pencil by stretching the arms and legs of 'K' and taking the first letters of 'IDEA' as the head. The simplicity adds a sense of efficiency which every office values.

Alex Dalmau

Photo: Susana Gellida
Agency: Larsson-Duprez
Client: DESKIDEA

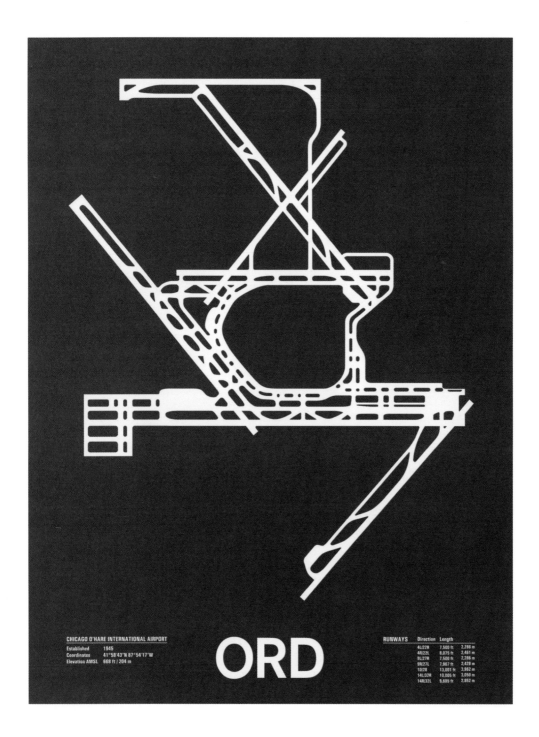

CHICAGO O'HARE INTERNATIONAL AIRPORT

Established	1945
Coordinates	41°58'43"N 87°54'17"W
Elevation AMSL	668 ft / 204 m

ORD

RUNWAYS	Direction	Length	
	4L/22R	7,500 ft	2,286 m
	4R/22L	8,075 ft	2,461 m
	9L/27R	7,500 ft	2,286 m
	9R/27L	7,967 ft	2,429 m
	10/28	13,001 ft	3,962 m
	14L/32R	10,005 ft	3,050 m
	14R/32L	9,685 ft	2,952 m

Airport Runway

Screenprinted posters picking out the beauty of prag-
matism and regional features that define the unique
structure of airport runways worldwide. Each track was
identified by a three-letter code and construction facts.

NOMO Design

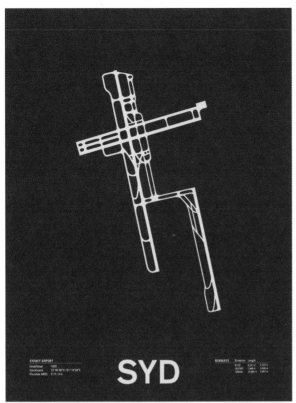

RUNWAYS	Direction	Length
07/25	8,301 ft	2,530 m
16L/34R	7,999 ft	2,438 m
16R/34L	13,000 ft	3,962 m

SYD

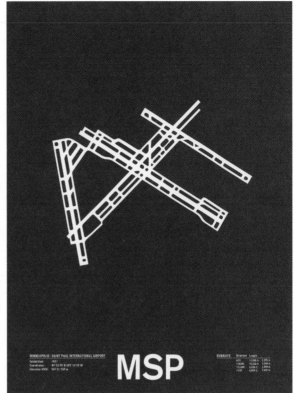

RUNWAYS	Direction	Length
4/22	11,006 ft	3,355 m
12R/30L	10,000 ft	3,048 m
12L/30R	8,200 ft	2,499 m
17/35	8,000 ft	2,439 m

MSP

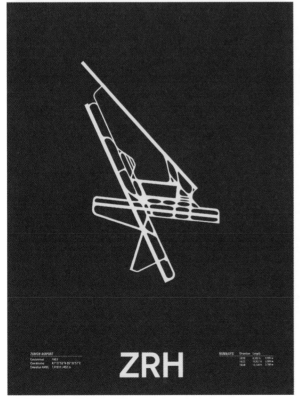

RUNWAYS	Direction	Length
10/28	8,201 ft	2,500 m
14/32	10,827 ft	3,300 m
16/34	12,139 ft	3,700 m

ZRH

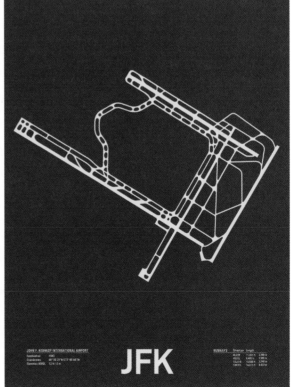

RUNWAYS	Direction	Length
4L/22R	11,351 ft	3,460 m
4R/22L	8,400 ft	2,560 m
13L/31R	10,000 ft	3,048 m
13R/31L	14,572 ft	4,442 m

JFK

Lost & Found

Selective entries to The Hello Poster
Show, a Seattle-based fundraising
exhibition. The theme of the Hello
Poster Show 2011 was to use merely
white on black to tell the audience to
"Get Lost!" and/or "Find Their Way".

The Hello Poster Show

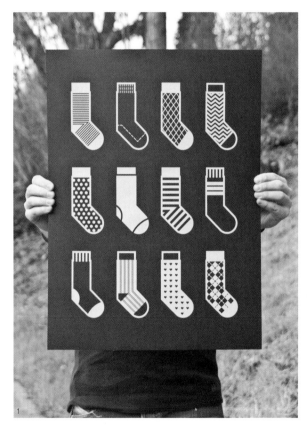

1. Lost & Found by Katrina Mendoza
2. Lost & Found by Jonny Sikov
3. Found by Tom Futrell
4. Lost by Jeff Wilkson
5. Lost by Nicholas Thiel
6. Lost by Jordan Evans, Travis Hosler
7. Found by Ethan Keller
8. Lost by Riley Hoonan

5

6

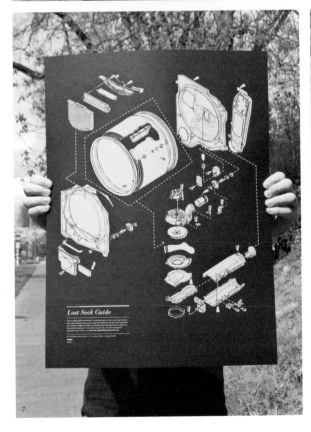

7

8

Limited

Printworks and notebooks with quirky quotes which Sennerholt came across in all parts of life. They do not necessarily appear in original words, and many were made up by Sennerholt herself.

Therese Sennerholt Design

Styling: Lotta Agaton
Photo: Pia Ulin, Henrik Bonnevier, Delight Studios

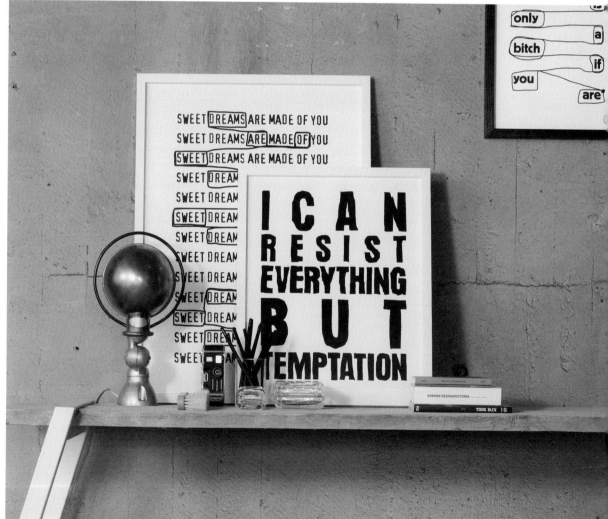

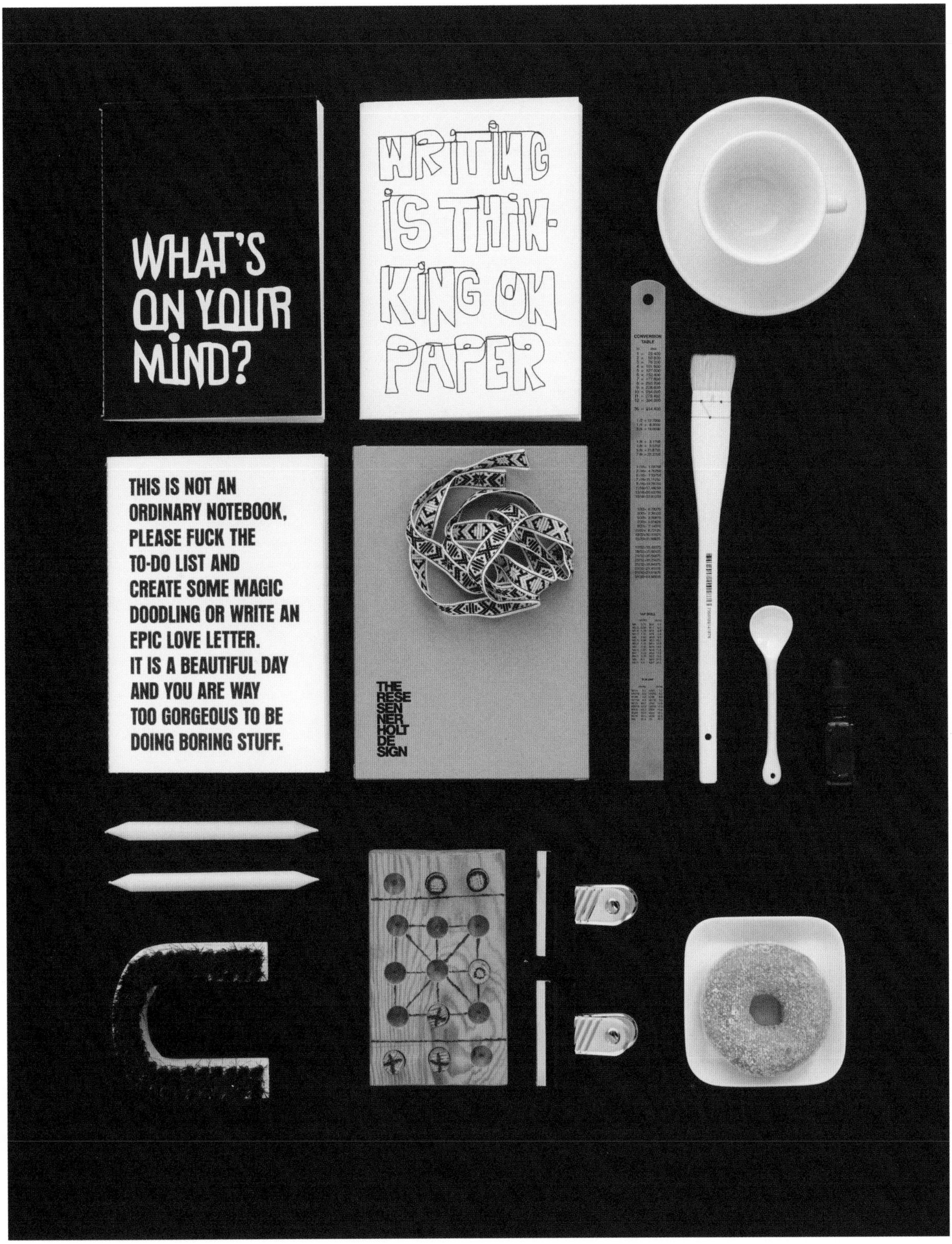

WHAT'S
ON YOUR
MIND?

WRITING
IS THIN-
KING ON
PAPER

THIS IS NOT AN
ORDINARY NOTEBOOK,
PLEASE FUCK THE
TO-DO LIST AND
CREATE SOME MAGIC
DOODLING OR WRITE AN
EPIC LOVE LETTER.
IT IS A BEAUTIFUL DAY
AND YOU ARE WAY
TOO GORGEOUS TO BE
DOING BORING STUFF.

THE
RESE
SEN
NER
HOLT
DE
SIGN

this is your space
an oasis where you can relax
take off your shoes
enjoy yourself and the art of living
feel free, think big, think small
this is a place where people will be seen
take your time and breathe
sense the moment, use your keys
and open your heart
laugh, cry or be crazy if you like
this is your space

WE PREFER THE BEAUTY OF CHAOS OVER UGLY PERFECTION

I EAT CAKE IN BED

IF IT MAKES YOU HAPPY DO IT, IF IT DOESN'T, THEN DON'T.

Be! Brave

you are the butter on my bread

I LOVE YOU MORE THAN MY TONGUE HAS EVER EXPRESSED

LIFE IS A PROGRESS AND NOT A STATION

HAPPY GUES LUCKY

IF **IT** MAKES YOU **HAPPY** DO IT, IF IT DOESN'T, THEN DON'T.

i HAVE NO DIRECTION IN MY LIFE AND i HAVE NEVER BEEN HAPPIER

  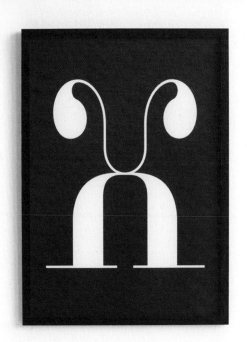

Spring

Instead of a bright colourful scene, it's a gloomy afternoon with spring shower, specially created for RVCA South Africa's The Guitar Show with "spring" as the theme. A gloss black was used to accent the floret subtly against its matte base.

Tokyo-Go-Go Illustration Studio

Photo: Roger Jardine (disturbance)
Project coordination: Melissa Williams (Blackbird Works)
Client: RVCA South Africa

Eames Chair

Two Eames LCW customised with types and graphics applied by hand. The words were inspired by a dialogue between Charles and Ray Eames at the Arlene Francis Home Show in 1956 as they unveiled the chair.

---

ilovedust

The Animal Chair Collection

Chair collection that connotes harmony and equality between human and animals. The realistic figures were CNC-machined from compressed foam, with seats upholstered in fine leather with a steel internal frame.

Maximo Riera

Marmalade Toast

Brandmark of upmarket café, TOAST, updated and
united with its parent company's moniker "Marmalade".
The new mark inherited the simplicity and quirk of its
vertical alignment in neutral colours to complement the
bright yellow interior of the café.

&Larry

Client: The Marmalade Group

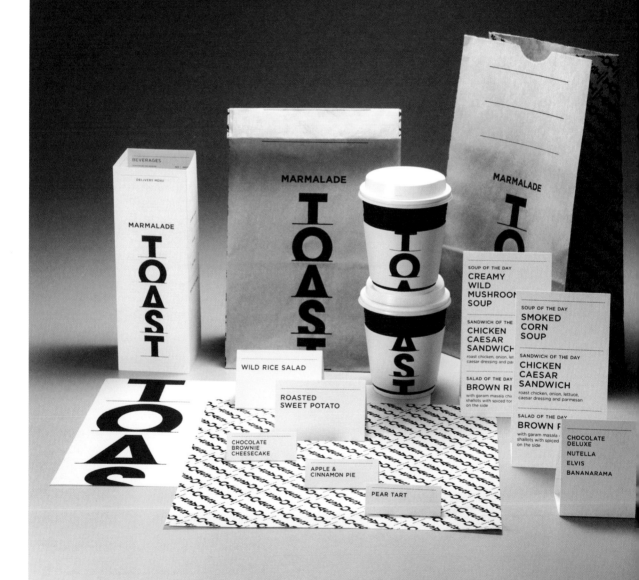

DELIVERY MENU

MARMALADE
TOAST

MARMALADE
TOAST

02-11 NGEE ANN CITY
391 ORCHARD ROAD

T 6733 8489
F 6733 6763

toast_nac@marmaladegroup.com

www.toast.com.sg

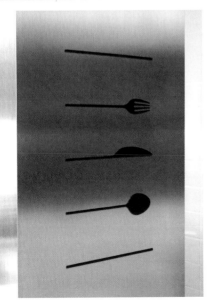

Oroton Windows

Window installations for Oroton's Asia Pacific stores. Oroton's luxury accessories were transformed into bright and luminous neon icons, interspersed with patterns and symbols that make fashion playfully chic.

Craig & Karl

Photo: Katherine Lu
Client: Oroton

"The distribution of the opposites allows viewers' eyes to bounce around the artwork, constantly resting on different focal points."

The Department Store

A modern take on traditional department store experience back in the early 1900s. From signage to collateral, the identity highlights the store's bold yet understated values with a sense of unity. Distinctive brand names were unified by TDS' house style and a lightbox.

Brogen Averill

Photo: Tom Roberton
Client: Karen Walker, Stephen Marr, Blackbox

JAMES
GN

01
LUCY & THE
POWDER ROOM

THE
DEPARTMENT
STORE

GIFT
VOUCHER

THE DEPARTMENT STORE

GF
KAREN
WALKER

THE
DEPARTMENT
STORE

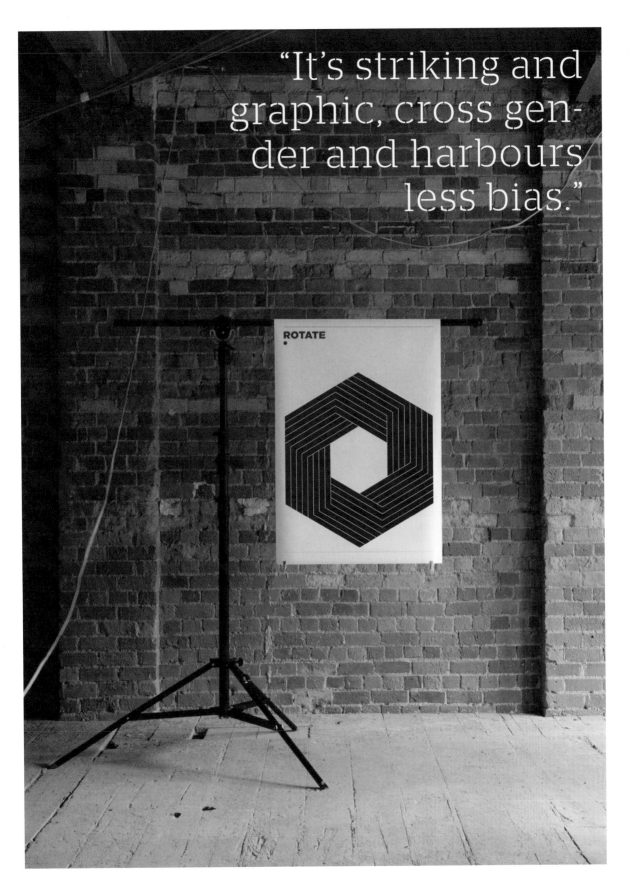

Watching Calendar

Wall calendar with days of each month set as the pupil and iris of human eyes on seperate sheets. Every two months, the eyes look at a different angle, just like Rawenstvo watching over clients' needs. It is Rawenstvo's gift for partners for on its 60th anniversary.

Graphic design studio by Yurko Gutsulyak

Illustration: Tatiana Trikoz
Client: JSC Rawenstvo

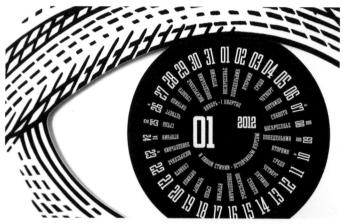

You Are The Ocean in Which I Learn To Swim

Typographic craft on a light box based around personal messages for The October Show at Salon91, Cape Town. The collective exhibition promised to be a meld of fine art, design and street art with a strong urban feel.

Jordan Metcalf

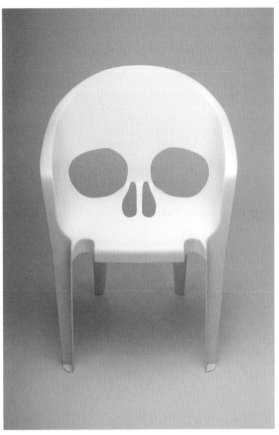

Souviens Toi Que
Tu Vas Mourir

A sarcastic remark on vanity. Named "*Remember That You Will Die*", the ubiquity of Monobloc chair and the symbolic meaning of skulls add up to a memento mori for those who seek comfort from the chair.

POOL

Photo: Benjamin Le Du

Visible Structures

Light and tough but easy to bend when used alone, carbon fibre shines as it becomes a subordinate material to give support. Here, the delicate polystyrene chair was fortified by the polymer adhered to its surface merely as broken stripes.

nendo
Photo: Masayuki Hayashi

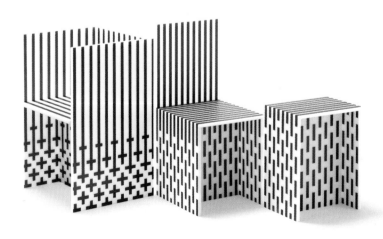

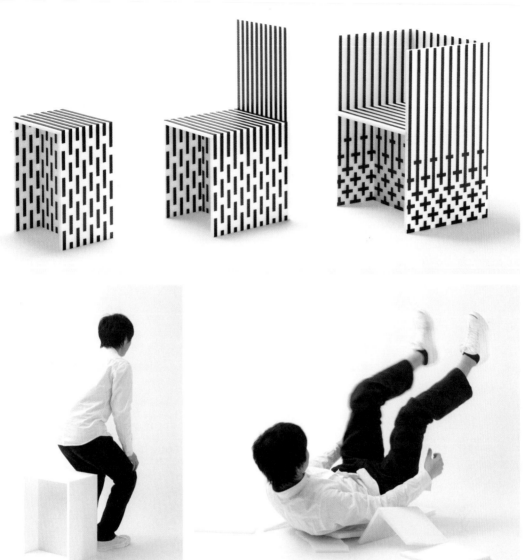

"We wanted to explore new possible expressions and accentuate the main material with carbon fibre in a supporting role, rather than as the star in its own right."

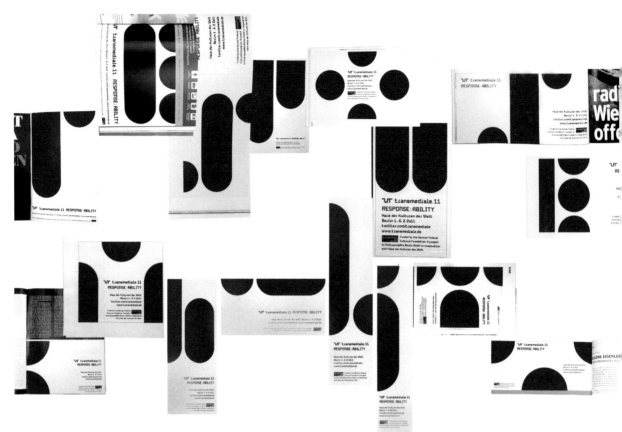

Transmediale.11

Promotional campaign for media art festival, Transmediale .11, probing into man-internet relationship, titled "RESPONSE:ABILITY". The graphic elements resemble '1' and '0' taken from the binary number system and DNA that can convey countless words and images.

+ Ruddigkeit

Client: Kulturprojekte Berlin GmbH

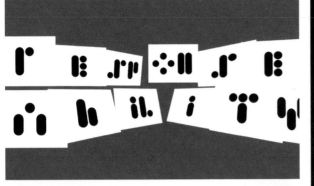

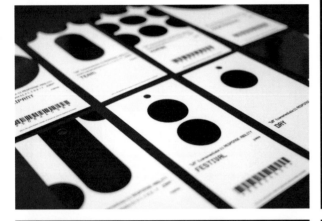

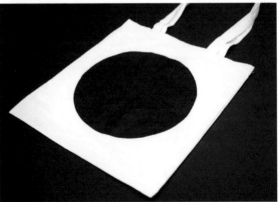

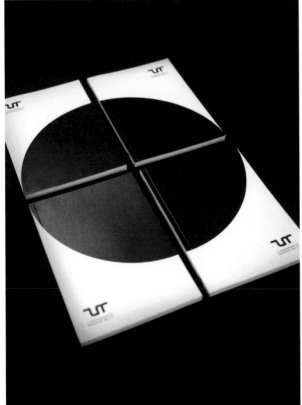

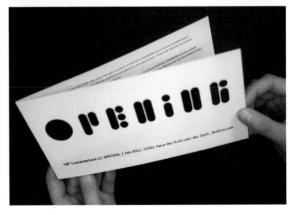

Gabbani

A fashionable and bold identity to set off the food and
wine offered at Gabbani, the oldest delicatessen in Swiss
city, Lugano. Visual references included flavour of the 30s
with mixed typefaces and optical art typical of the 60s.

DEMIAN CONRAD DESIGN
Client: Gabbani

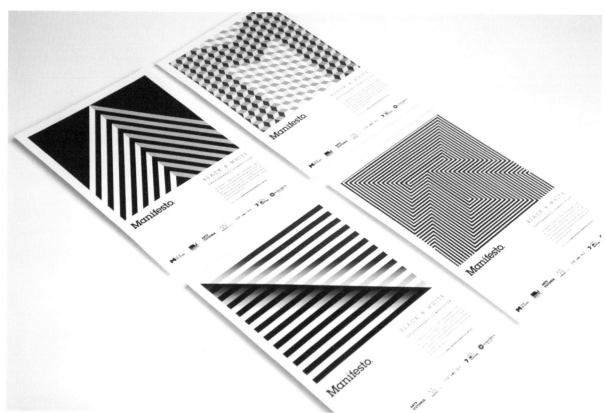

Manifesto.

Visual identity for Manifesto., a black-and-white photo competition for undergraduates in Melbourne. Op art elements were exploited to give a subtle sense of movement and distinction between illusions and pictures, as well as understanding and seeing.

Josip Kelava
Client: Manifesto.

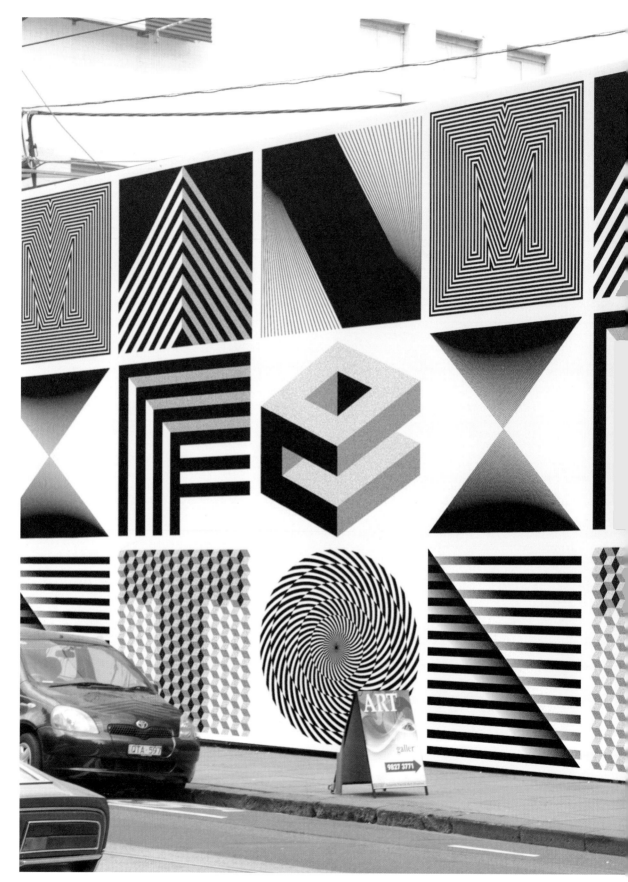

200 Aldersgate

Wayfinding system and identity based on clean lines and an assured palette to embrace the physicality of the 1960s modular office block and new visions as it transformed into the new 200 Aldersgate.

dn&co.

Client: Helical Bar

200
ALDERSGATE
BIKE STORE

Too Big To Fail

A black helium balloon measuring 150cm in diameter, handpainted with white letters installed for exhibition, grafik12, in Zurich. "Too Big To Fail" commented on the phrase's frequent appearance in economic and financial policies.

Studio Marcus Kraft

"To create a silent contrast to the rest of the exhibition, it was obvious to use black and white."

4 280 630

98 057

3 246 727

3 007 142

2 378 918

2 498 392

Arbeitslosigkeit
Unemployment

1 868 504

1 073 576

459 499

154 923

152

Statistics Strip

An extensive narrative stripe and axis running through exhibition, Work. Meaning and Concern, at German Hygiene Museum. Apart from graphics, the band linked up and related the materials at various levels by means of rotary knobs and with integrated touchscreens showing interviews.

ART+COM

Scenography: chezweitz und roseapple
Curation: Praxis für Ausstellung und Theorie
[Hürlimann | Lepp | Tyradellis]
Client: Deutsches Hygiene-Museum Dresden

0 %

hen

Violent crime

International statistics on violent crime need to be taken with a pinch of salt, as every country defines and registers crime differently. Regardless of this, the attempt to remove the causes of violence and crime, primarily social inequality and extreme poverty for example, is one of the great challenges before us. One important means for doing so is work: work absorbs aggression and gives individuals the feeling they can actively shape their own lives and the societies they live in.

Trinkwasser

Was für uns selbstverständlich ist, ist in manchen Regionen der Erde eine Frage um Leben oder Tod: der Zugang zu sauberen Trinkwasser. Experten gehen davon aus, dass in Wassermangel ein wesentlicher Grund für kriegerische Auseinandersetzungen in der Zukunft liegen wird. Der Erhalt, die Herstellung und Verteilung der Ressource Wasser gehört müßten zu einem der drängendsten Arbeitsfelder.

Drinking water

Something we take for granted is a matter of life and death in some regions of the earth: access to clean drinking water. Experts anticipate that water shortages will be a major cause of war and conflict in the years to come. Preserving, producing and distributing water as a resource is one of the most urgent tasks facing us.

Arbeitslosen

2005 sind weltweit 2.85 Milliarden Menschen einer
Tätigkeit nachgegangen. Die absolute Zahl erwerbs-
tätiger Menschen erhöht sich kontinuierlich. Aufgr...
noch stärker wachsenden Bevölkerungszahl nimmt...
der relative Anteil der Beschäftigten an der Gesam...
rung stetig ab. Ungeachtet dessen bleibt Arbeit w...
eine der wichtigsten Möglichkeiten, seine Lebens...
und seine soziale Stellung zu verbessern.

zu Bildung   Access to education

...ehört zu den wesentlichen
...amt zur Möglichkeit, an-
...e Berufe zu erlernen. Bei den
...n international noch große
...n zu den unmittelbaren
...hört.

Reading and writing skills are key requirements for education,
and thus for the opportunity to learn complex activities and
occupations. In international comparison, there are still major
differences in the educational opportunities available. Rectify-
ing this imbalance is among the most pressing tasks of the
near future.

Lebenserwartung   Life expectancy

...tatistisch betrachtet werden die Menschen immer älter.
...harzus erwächst die Notwendigkeit, den Lebensunterhalt
...von immer mehr Menschen gleichzeitig zu gewährleisten.
...Dabei unterscheiden sich die Lebenserwartungen auf der
...Welt zum Teil gewaltig. Gründe hierfür liegen vor allem
...in der unterschiedlichen Versorgung mit Nahrung und Medi-
...zin, aber auch in den grundsätzlichen Lebens- und Arbeits-
...bedingungen sowie der Gefahr, Krieg und Gewalt ausgesetzt
...zu sein.

From a statistical perspective, people are getting older and
older. This means we have to ensure that more and more
people have the means to survive at the same time. Yet life
expectancy is very varied around the world. This is mainly
due to differing access to food and medicine, but also...
basic living and working conditions and the risk of...
posed to war and violence.

Shizuoka City
Museum of Art

Established as a place for the exchange of
views on arts, Shizoka City Museum of Art
emphasises the importance of seeing with
different points of view. The visual system and
posters complement the institute's interior
with hairline graphics and customised type.

10inc.
Client: Shizuoka City Museum Of Art

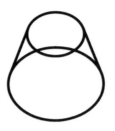

JR静岡駅北口
葵タワー3階

開館記念展10月より

5〜9月までは講演会や
ワークショップ等を随時開催

開館時間 10:00−19:00 月曜休館
5月1日（土）は12時開館

静岡市美術館
SHIZUOKA CITY
MUSEUM of ART

静岡市美術館
SHIZUOKA CITY
MUSEUM of ART

静岡市美術館
SHIZUOKA CITY
MUSEUM of ART

静岡市美術館
SHIZUOKA CITY
MUSEUM of ART

2010年5月1日（土）開館

静岡市美術館 〒420-0852 静岡市葵区紺屋町17-1葵タワー3F Aoi Tower 3F, 17-1, Kouya-machi, Aoi-ku, Shizuoka, 420-0852 JAPAN tel. 059-273-1515 fax. 059-273-1518 www.shizubi.jp

Moscow Design Museum

Visual identity for Russia's first mobile museum with focuses on graphic design. The geometric figures refer to Russian crystals, a unique heritance from Russian design history.

Lava

Client: Moscow Design Museum

 МОСКОВСКИЙ МУЗЕЙ ДИЗАЙНА MOSCOW DESIGN MUSEUM

 МОСКОВСКИЙ МУЗЕЙ ДИЗАЙНА MOSCOW DESIGN MUSEUM

 МОСКОВСКИЙ МУЗЕЙ ДИЗАЙНА MOSCOW DESIGN MUSEUM

 МОСКОВСКИЙ МУЗЕЙ ДИЗАЙНА MOSCOW DESIGN MUSEUM

МОСКОВСКИЙ МУЗЕЙ ДИЗАЙНА
MOSCOW DESIGN MUSEUM

Александра Санькова
организатор
ALEXANDRA SANKOVA
FOUNDER

T +7 926 245 9033
E SANKOVA@MOSCOWDESIGNMUSEUM.RU
W WWW.MOSCOWDESIGNMUSEUM.RU

МОСКОВСКИЙ МУЗЕЙ ДИЗАЙНА
MOSCOW DESIGN MUSEUM

Надежда Бакурадзе
организатор
NADEZHDA BAKURADZE
FOUNDER

T +7 926 264 6686
E BAKURADZE@MOSCOWDESIGNMUSEUM.RU
W WWW.MOSCOWDESIGNMUSEUM.RU

МОСКОВСКИЙ МУЗЕЙ ДИЗАЙНА
MOSCOW DESIGN MUSEUM

Валерий Патконен
организатор
VALERY PATKONEN
FOUNDER

T +7 495 729 7302
E PATKONEN@MOSCOWDESIGNMUSEUM.RU
W WWW.MOSCOWDESIGNMUSEUM.RU

Boxpark

Boxpark is a new pop-up mall fabricated from over 60 recycled sea cans in Shoreditch, the UK. Minimal colours compliment the brutal shipping containers with exaggerated types and patterns to create dramatic gestures for the noval shopping mode.

StudioMakgill

Photo: Guy Archard
Client: Boxpark

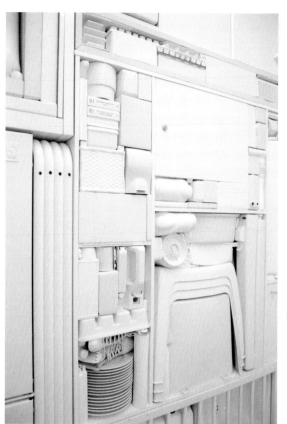
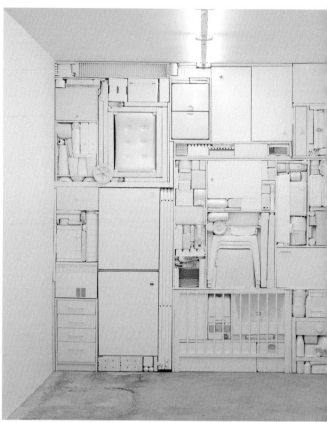

Ghost

Site-specific installations methodically erected to fill up the odd space in the architecture of exhibition space. The original purposes of objects were forced into submission, leaving shades of white that can only be reckoned as a wall.

Michael Johansson
Client: Galleri Arnstedt (Östra Karup),
The Flat – Massimo Carasi (Milan)

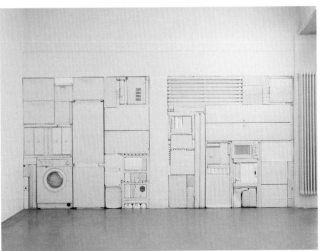

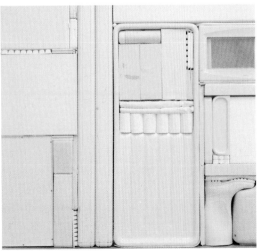

"In a broad sense, all objects within the installation can be described as white, but in the context the gradations towards blue, red or yellow suddenly become clear when seen one by one."

Thin Black Lines/Dancing Squares

Like flowing water, the handdrawn lines on the floorboard
set off nendo's furniture collections in two exhibition rooms.
The opposite colourways accentuate the respective concepts,
"still black" and "active white".

nendo

Photo: Daici Ano

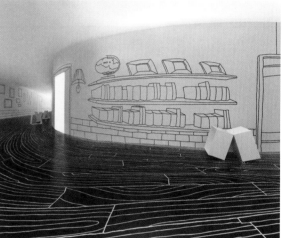

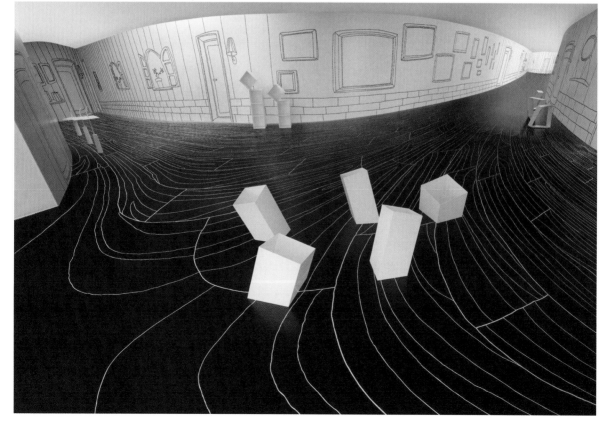

NY 11-18-02-10

dunhill's pop-up store at New York Fashion Week 2010,
recreating an ethereal facade of Bourdon House where
Alfred Dunhill lives. The marriage of black and white
allows light and shade to blend in harmoniously with
dramatic effect.

Campaign

Lighting/ photo: Frank Oudeman
Client: dunhill

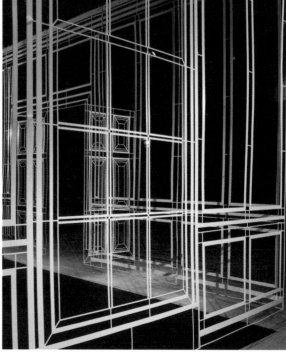

Eyecharts

A personal attempt of setting out an op art installaion, with shapes camouflaged with its surrounding. While patterns and shapes merge with one another, traits of eye charts acted as a cue for its connection to vision.

Alexander Kent

Set design: Lightning and Kinglyface
Special credits: We Folk

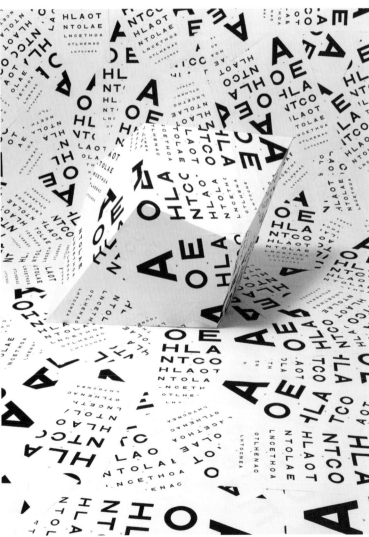

Forms in Space

Stripping away colours, Stocker's extensive installations play on lines, structures and surfaces to shake viewers' perception of space as they walk inside. Foam core, masking tape, wood, acrylic and pins are the basic materials that found Stocker's work.

Esther Stocker

Photo: 1-altrospazio, 2-Ondrej Polak, 3-Esther Stocker, 4-Jan Mahr, 5-Martin Pardatscher, 6-Loredana Ginocchio

3

4

5

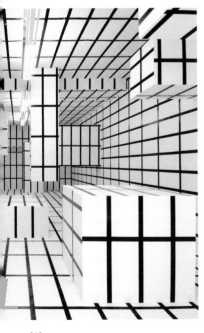

Biography

&Larry

Whether commercial or experimental, &Larry approaches each project with a desire to create works that are honest, functional and expressive beyond aesthetics. The studio has adopted the Eames motto of "Take your pleasure seriously" and this philosophy can be seen in a diverse body of work that includes film posters as well as a series of intriguing Singapore-inspired Objects.

P. 198-199

+ Ruddigkeit

Born in Leipzig in 1968, illustrator, designer, and art director Raban Ruddigkeit founded his own agency in Berlin in 2009. A member of the ADC and a Boardmember of Create Berlin, Ruddigkeit has won around 100 national and international awards. In 2012, his agency was awarded as "Rookie Agency of the year" from ADC Germany and the KfW Cashgroup.

P. 212-213

10inc.

Founded by award-winning graphic designer and art director Masahiro Kakinokihara in 2007, 10inc. is a Tokyo-based design studio focusing on branding, graphic design, advertising and poster design.

P. 230-231

A3 Collectif

Founded by Yvo Hählen and Priscilla Balmer in 2011, the Lausanne-based studio is specialised in branding, editorial design, illustration and poster design. The team also works on creative publishing, record cover and label. Animated by the same impulses, A3 regularly participates in events of illustration, street art and has exhibited in many galleries.

P. 046, 068-069

Acne JR

A special branch from the Acne Family company group founded in 1996, the Stockholm-based toy company aims to create traditional, iconic toys in a modern way that is also eco-friendly and inspiring for children.

P. 042-045

ART+COM

Building upon the foundation of the ex-experimental design organisation formed by the Berlin University of Arts, ART+COM was officially became a design studio in 1998 aiming to explore art, science and technology, in order to create innovative, unexpected, risky and experimental projects, and to pursue the beauty of precise and delicacy.

P. 226-229

ARTIVA DESIGN

Located in Genoa, Italy, since 2003, ARTIVA DESIGN is founded by Daniele De Batté and Davide Sossi focusing in visual art, graphics, illustration and multimedia.

P. 047, 073, 080, 117, 139-141

Asylum

A creative company comprises of a design studio, a retail store, a workshop and a record label. Since their inception in 1999, Asylum has worked on cross disciplinary projects that include interactive design, product development, environmental and interior design, packaging, apparel design, branding and graphic design.

P. 102-103, 168-169

Atelier BangBang

Founded by Simon Laliberté from Montreal, Quebec, Canada who graduated in graphic design at UQAM, Montreal, the studio specialises in branding, packaging, illustration and print design.

P. 038-039

Atelier Christian von der Heide

Specialising in product, corporate logo and editorial design, Heide received a Red Dot Design Award in 2010 and was nominated for the German Design Award in 2011. After collaborating and sharing a studio with renowned designer Peter Schmidt, he opened his own studio in Hamburg and Berlin in 2010. His clients include institutions Strellson and 4711 as well as international celebrities such as Dita Von Teese and Michael Michalsky.

P. 064

Atipus

Barcelona-based graphic communication studio specialises in corporate identity, art direction, packaging design, editorial and web services, Atipus has been continually awarded by National and European design honours including Laus Awards, ADC°E Awards and Anuaria.

P. 050

Averill, Brogen

A New Zealand-based graphic designer who works in a wide range of design projects from branding to signage, packaging to web. Before he moved back to New Zealand in 2004, he had been worked in design agencies in London and Paris.

P. 202-205

Barton, John

Graduated from Leeds Metropolitan University recently, the British graphic designer is now freelancing for numberous well-established UK based-studios. Specialising in graphic design, branding, and typography, he enjoys to make handcraft screen printing work, taking up both commissioned work and independent projects.

P. 100-101, 142-143

BERG

An independent UK-based ideas studio. Design seamlessly across a wide range of interdisciplinary media including prints, screen and the environment, BERG has an international reputation for innovation, imagination, and sound commercial values working closely with clients and industry professionals to create solutions that are considered, engaging and effective.

P. 106-107

Berger & Föhr

Exists to support businesses, organizations, and brands dedicated to the development of socially and environmentally responsible products, ideas, information and assets, the Corlorado-based multidisciplinary design studio is specialised in delivering strategy and art direction, identity design and brand-building, website and application design, print and collateral design, illustration, symbols, icons, pictograms and environmental graphic design.

P. 130-131

BLOW

Established by Ken Lo in 2010, who graduated from HKU SPACE Community College in Visual Communication and won the Champion of "Design Student of The Year", BLOW specialises in identity and branding, packaging, print, publications, environmental graphics and website design.

P. 022-023, 062-063

Bonnevier, Johanna

Based in East London, the Swedish art director, graphic designer and illustrator graduated at Central Saint Martins and Camberwell College of Art and Design. A member of design collective weare42, she works closely for the fashion industry on graphic design, show/ window installation, and editorial design in addition to a wide range of architecture and culture based projects.

P. 082, 092-093

Borka, Todd

A French illustrator working for both youth literature and magazines, Borka likes mixing the aesthetic of Indian ink with the multiplicity of possibilities offered by image editing software.

P. 030

Bossuet, Emmanuel

French graphic artist and creative director first set into the industrial design field and worked for the multimedia group TCL hybrid design electronic product branch Tim Thom design studio at the late 90s, Bossuet later found interest in fashion and started to create pattern and print alongside his product design practice. He then set up the EEM Studio working closely with worldwide luxurious fashion brands.

P. 094-095

Bravo&Tango

Founded by London-based graphic designer Dan Osman who recently starts working freelance after few years of solid experience in marketing and advertising agencies. He works mainly in brand identities, literature, typography, editorial pieces and web-based media.

P. 076-077

Bunch

A leading London-based design studio specialising in identity, literature, editorial, digital and motion, Bunch has been working with world class brands like BBC, Nike, Diesel, Sony, Sky, and Red Bull for a decade.

P. 152-153

C100 Purple Haze

A Munich-based multidisciplinary design consultancy founded by Christian Hundertmark and Clemens Baldermann working for miscellaneous public and private clients on a variety of national and international projects including conception, art direction, typography, design and illustration delivering inventive and precise visual solutions.

P. 084

Campaign

The London-based award-winning retail design agency is one of the best specialists in developing integral brand experience by a comprehensive package of interior, brand and digital design. The team consists talents from a diverse range of backgrounds including architects, film makers, interior, graphic and product designers.

P. 242-243

Case Studyo

Launched by TOYKYO, Case Studyo is a producer and publisher of contemporary artist series with dedicated focus and ambition aiming to publish limited and open edition objects and artworks with a striking visual language.

P. 034-035

Caserne

Ugo Varin-Lachapelle, aka Caserne, is a 25 years old graphic designer from Montreal, Quebec.

P. 041

Coco

A successful communication consultant in fashion with five years fine arts background in Paris. Coco later moved to London and set up a creative and technology consultancy, getConfused, in 2004. Besides her own label Forget-Me-Not, Coco also creates imagery for major retail brands and international publications like Vogue, ELLE, Nylon and Muse.

Her work has been published in numerous publications including Taschen, Gestalten, Viction:ary and several exhibitions in London, Los Angeles and Barcelona.

www.cocopit.biz

P. 096-099

COMMUNE

A creative team based in Sapporo, Japan who specialises in graphic design. Motivated by the will to make things better, COMMUNE works to encourage people and the society for a change. At times, their creations take people by surprise, awaken their emotions, or even move them to tears.

P. 014-015, 074

Company

Founded in 2006, the London-based graphic design studio with a focus on visual identity takes a tactile and simple approach believing that the most successful outcomes contain strong ideas with a playful twist, Company has been awarded at the Greek Design & Illustration Awards and has been exhibited at the BFI Southbank, the ICA, the European Design Awards and the Royal College of Art, amongst others.

P. 018-019

Craig & Karl

Based in two cities across the ocean, Craig & Karl is a design duo formed by Craig Redman and Karl Maier. Signature in the colourful, geometric pattern face, they work on projects in various medium including murals, sculpture, illustration, installation, interface design, typography, iconography, fabric patterns and print. They have exhibited internationally in many countries, most notably at the Musé de la Publicité, Louvre.

P. 200-201

Dalmau, Alex

An art director based in Barcelona, Dalmau specialises in graphic design, branding and corporate identity. After graduating from the Image and Design School (IDEP), he worked at various advertising agencies and design studios like Animal-BCN, Larsson-Duprez, Creatica and began working as a freelance in 2011. His clients include Progess, Mandarin Oriental Barcelona, Carolina Herrera, Adidas, Ricola, Font Vella, Reig Capital and many others.

P. 178-181

Del Valle, Cesar

A recent graduate in Arts at the Universidad de Antioquia, Medellin in 2010, Del Valle's work has been exhibited extensively both locally and internationally since 2006.

P.146-147

DEMIAN CONRAD DESIGN

Founded in 2007, the multidisciplinary studio works mainly in the cultural field and the leisure industry focusing on events communication and visual identity. Based in Lausanne and Bellinzona, the team is always keen to work with clients who would like to play a full role in the creative process.

P.214-217

dn&co.

Run by directors Ben Dale and Joy Nazzari, the London-based creative agency works with international property funds, developers and agents to achieve fresh and effective brand, marketing and communications strategies.

P.222-223

Dowling, Marie-Niamh

An independent graphic designer currently based in Mainz, Germany, Dowling has recently graduated in Communication Design at HS-RM, Wiesbaden.

P.144-145

Edited

Established in 2011 by Wu Cheuk-pan, Renatus, the Hong Kong-based studio specialises in publication and identity design.

P.132-133

Emily Forgot

The moniker of London-based designer and illustrator Emily Alston who graduated from Liverpool School of Art and Design in 2004. Approaching all briefs with creative thought, originality, humour and beauty in mind, Emily Forgot works to develop her own range of products as well as commercial projects for clients big and small.

P.028, 124-125

Eumann, Jan

Graduated at the FH Düsseldorf, Germany with a year experience working for Wolff Olins' different offices as intern and junior designer, Eumann then joined Peter Schmidt Group and as well worked as freelancer with DMCGroup and Interbrand. In 2012, Eumann gets back to Wolff Olins New York as a senior designer.

P.088-091

FEB Design

A multidisciplinary design collective based in Oporto, Portugal since 2009.

P.174-175

FEIXEN: Design by Felix Pfäffli

Founded after graduated at Lucerne School of Graphic Design in 2010, the Swiss graphic designer has started to teach typography, narrative design and poster design in 2011. His work is widely recognised among the international design community.

P.172-173

Ferencz, Miklós

Believing that graphic design is a great tool to understand the world, the graphic designer keeps learning and experimenting after he graduated in graphic design at Visart Academy in Budapest. He worked for a PR company for two years before he went to the Netherlands for his MA degree in graphic design at St. Joost Academy, Breda. Currently, he is studying another master degree at Moholy-Nagy Arts and Design University, Budapest.

P.065

FIBA Design

A design studio specialises in products, identities, publications, posters, books, exhibitions, websites, and signage systems.

P.174-175

filthymedia

Established in 2004, filthymedia works for a wide range of clients and sectors, from music to fashion. Their portfolio includes graphic design, art direction, branding, typography, web & motion design, illustration, photography and copyrighting.

P.024-025

Fons Hickmann m23

Founded in 2001 by Gesine Grotrian-Steinweg and Fons Hickmann, the Berlin-based studio focuses on communication systems from print to cross media design. It is among today's most awarded design studios worldwide.

P.078-079

Garrett, Michael

The freelancer is specialised in graphic and web design, identity, promotional materials, marketing, creative writing and socially responsible design practices.

P.051

Graphic design studio by Yurko Gutsulyak

Born in 1979 in Ukraine with an academic background in economics, Gutsulyak began his design career in 2001 and founded the studio in 2005. His work has been widely published and exhibited internationally such as France, Poland and China. The winner of more than 30 international awards was elected as the first president of Art Directors Club Ukraine in 2010.

P.206-207

Greece is for Lovers

A product design boutique founded by Thanos Karampatsos and Christina Kotsilelou introducing the natural sense of "Greekness" to contemporary product design, the studio sets their base in a souvenir shop at Acropolis in Athens, targeting to promote Greek culture and design through the exquisite products.

P.031, 056-057

Hansen, Michael

Currently a student in visual communication at the Royal Danish Academy of Fine Arts School of Design, Hansen primarily works with conceptual ideas that explore the world of graphic design, fashion photography, and visual identity design.

P.072

Happycentro

Founded in 1998 in Verona, Happycentro has worked for both big and small clients since then. Mixing complexity, order and fatigue is their formula for beauty. In addition to the commissioned work, the team always spend plenty of energy in research and testing on visual art, typography, graphic design, illustration, animation, film direction and music.

P.020-021

Hasenstaub, Lívia

Born in Serbia, Hasenstaub is a young graphic designer from Budapest, Hungary. Currently studying at University of Applied Arts Vienna on scholarship, she is interested in typography and geometrical forms.

P.065

HelloMe

A Berlin-based design studio focuses on art direction, graphic design and typography. With a systematic design approach, HelloMe creates and implements innovative communication strategies and distinctive dynamic visual systems for cultural, social and business clients.

P.170-171

Here Design

Founded by Kate Marlow, Caz Hildebrand and Mark Paton in 2005, the multidisciplinary design collective specialises in design and strategic thinking for branding, packaging, print, publishing, point-of-sale, products and websites. They have been nominated and awarded in several local and international awards, including D&AD, V&A Illustration Awards and Pentaward.

P.113

Hovercraft Studio

Renamed as Hovercraft from Second World Design in 2011, the visual identity specialist works on a wide range of design projects from print to interactive, illustration to product branding. They are currently based in Portland.

P.075

Ibán Ramón + Dídac Ballester

After running their own studios for several years, the duo has joined forces to work on design and graphic communication, as well as experimental and research projects.

P.128-129

ilovedust

A multidisciplinary design boutique specialises in creative solutions from graphic design and illustration to animation and trend prediction. ilovedust plies their trade in two contrasting locations in East London and the south coast of England where the blend of two provides them a unique and inspiring perspective.

P.195

Information Architects

Split up into two operation units based in Zurich and Tokyo, the interactive design agency is founded by Oliver Reichenstein and Chris Lüscher focusing on interface design and digital typography.

P.108-109

Johansson, Michael

After finishing studies in Norway and Germany, Johansson returned to Sweden and took his master degree at Malmö Art Academy in 2005. He has taken part in several residencies and exhibited frequently both within and outside of Sweden.

P.148-149, 236-239

Karpavičius, Tadas

Originally from Lithuania, Karpavičius, the London-based versatile graphic designer and visual artist specialise in typography, publication, printed matter, moving image and photography. Paper cutout illustration and collage are slso his signature work.

P.010, 081

Kasper Pyndt Studio

A young graphic designer from Copenhagen, Denmark who is studying at The Royal Danish Academy of Fine Arts School of Design, while also working with the multidisciplinary design studio, Make. Pyndt's work takes basis in a strong sense of concept and minimalism. He always strives to reinvent himself with involvement of experimental typography or illustration.

P.070-071

Kasper, Larissa and Florio, Rosario

Based in St. Gallen, Switzerland, the two graphic designers with a strong focus on typography have been collaborating for various projects mainly on printed matter for the musical and cultural field mostly. Together with a couple of friends, they share a studio named Collective in St.Gallen.

P.066-067, 104-105, 110-111, 123, 165

Kelava, Josip

Having graduated at Swinburne Faculty of Design, the Croatian-born designer focuses on graphic design, typography and photog-

raphy. He is currently working for Clemenger BBDO as a full-time Senior Designer.

P.218-221

Kent, Alexander

The British photographer found his interest in photography since he was young and began studying photography at Plymouth College of Art and Design at the age of 16. After studying at Blackpool and Fylde College, he moved his base to London and worked closely in the fashion industry. Later, he set up the studio Bethnal Green, focusing more on still life photography.

P.244-245

Lava

Based in Amsterdam and founded in 1990, design agency Lava has strong roots in editorial design. Working as visual storytellers over the years has led to a unique approach to identity and communication design. The diverse team of graphic, motion and interactive designers works for a diverse range of clients from the commercial, governmental, non-profit and cultural sector.

P.232-233

Leterme Dowling

The multidisciplinary design studio with a global client base works closely and openly with clients from the outset on projects of all scales across a variety of applications from logos, websites, promotional literature and identity systems, to brochures, packaging and signage.

P.058-061

Lo Siento

Graduated at London College of Communication (London Institute) in 2003, Borja Martinez set up the agency in 2004 in Barcelona working in a wide range of projects from packaging, music covers, editorial design, graphic identities for restaurants and film production companies.

P.040

Mark Brooks Graphik Design

Working between New York and Barcelona on a broad range of projects for diverse international clients, the graphic designer is devoted into a number of personal design projects which he conveys graphic design, typography and visual communication.

P.085

Biography

Metcalf, Jordan

Based in Cape Town, South Africa, Metcalf loves typography, illustration, good design and the combination of the aforementioned.

P. 208

Murmure

The creative communication agency overturns the limits between art, graphic design and communication via the awakening of senses, poetry and elegance of textures, creating original and efficient communications.

P. 016-017, 158-163

nendo

Founded by architect Oki Sato in 2002 in Tokyo, nendo holds its goal of bringing small surprises to people through multidisciplinary practices of different media including architecture, interiors, furniture, industrial products and graphic design.

P. 210-211, 240-241

Nieminen, Lotta

Currently based in New York, Nieminen is a multidisciplinary Finnish designer and illustrator from Helsinki. After studying graphic design and illustration at the University of Art and Design Helsinki and the Rhode Island School of Design, she becomes a freelancer in both fields since 2006.

P. 126-127

NOMO Design

A multidisciplinary creative studio based in Chicago, Illinois, NOMO is founded in 2010 by architect and designer Jerome Daksiewicz providing a full range of design services including identity, graphic, environmental, information and interaction design. Through intent listening, research and questioning, the studio works closely with clients to craft meaningful, strategic and integrated design solutions.

P. 182-183

Non-Format

Established in London in 2000 by Kjell Ekhorn and Jon Forss, the two-man team works on a diverse range of projects including art direction, design, illustration and custom typography for a list of international brands. Forss relocated to Minneapolis, USA and, in 2009, Ekhorn returned to his native Norway. Skype™ becomes the bridge for them to work together on every project.

P. 054-055

Not Available

A multidisciplinary studio providing creative ideas for design strategy, art direction, interactive media as well as space design. N/A believes that "Design" is not a solo game that provides just a single style in different tasks; yet, every party plays an important role in the creative process to accomplish a great work. No individualism is available.

P. 052-053

Pastor, Joan Ramon

Spanish graphic designer, Joan Ramon Pastor, a.k.a. Wete, paints graffitis with a passion on typography since his childhood. Pastor is currently based in Barcelona and working at Vasava.

P. 086-087

POKETO

An online destination born out of a belief in "art for your everyday" for design-driven wares that takes art off the gallery walls and into people's lives, Founded by Ted Vadakan and Angie Myung in 2003, the husband-and-wife team has just opened its first retail/gallery in downtown Los Angeles.

P. 029

POOL

Founded by Léa Padovani and Sébastien Kieffer in 2010, POOL is a collective concept based on "outside the box" thinking. They design objects that are off-beat, dreamlike, at times melancholy, while always remaining functional.

P. 209

Poulain, Damien

The graphic designer and art director has been working in a wide range of fields but more specifically for art, fashion and music projects in London since 2002. Poulain is also the founder of publishing house, oodee, whose books have been recognised by the photography community for their outstanding design and art direction.

P. 049

Poulsen, Mads Jakob

Recognized by the likes of D&AD, IF Award, Print Magazine and Creative Circle Award, the Danish designer was ranked the top 50 designers of the world list by Art Directors Club New York in 2010, making him an ADC Young Gun. Poulsen is currently a senior designer at Wolff Olins in New York.

P. 120-121

Raffinerie AG für Gestaltung

Established in 2000, the studio is managed by Reto Ehrbar, Nenad Kovačić and Christian Haas with a talented team of graphic artists and illustrators.

P. 112

Ribeiro, Rui

Having studied in both Portugal and the UK, Ribeiro has worked at Hyperakt, New York for clients on cultural and social change. He also had a brief experience at COLORS Magazine in Italy. He is now a freelancer working mostly on print and typography.

P. 118-119, 122

Riera, Maximo

Based in Cadiz, Riera is a practicing artist for over 30 years. Whilst predominantly working in photography, painting and sculpture, Riera has also published a collection of poetry. Apart from his professional life in the medical industry, Riera organised several exhibitions and events for his work, with all proceeds going to charity.

P. 196-197

Root

Based in London, the multidisciplinary design studio founded by Martin Root in 1990 works to deliver innovative and effective solutions for a diverse, worldwide client base. The studio provides services in design, art direction, advertising and motion pictures.

P. 166-167

ruiz+company

Led by David Ruiz, the team specialises in creating innovative brand concepts and codes, corporate identity, advertising, packaging and broadcast design. They have been honoured with more than 100 national and international awards.

P. 150-151

Smel

Founded in 2001 by Edgar Smaling and Carlo Elias, Smel for Smel creative and strategic design studio consists of a dynamic team of dedicated, multidisciplinary creative people specialising in strategic corporate identities, magazines, books, websites, as well as illustrious design concepts which subtly unite quality and imagination.

Stocker, Esther

The award-winning Italian artist is best known for her large scale geometric and line installations which create a sense of clean and abstract spatial perception. She has launched numerous solo exhibitions and participated in an impressive amount of group shows internationally since 1995.

Studio Astrid Stavro

Graduated with distinction from The Royal College of Art in 2005, Stavro works for international clients and numerous publishing houses since then. She co-runs the publishing house Infolio, lectures internationally and teaches editorial design at IDEP. The studio's work has been featured extensively in the press and won more than 90 international awards. The member of Alliance Graphique Internationale (AGI), Stavro also writes for various journals such as Grafik and Creative Review and is a contributing editor of Elephant magazine.

Studio Marcus Kraft

An award-winning graphic design office based in Zurich, Switzerland and works on diversified disciplines including art direction, design, concept and typography with an emphasis on elaborated design concepts, editorial projects and typographical quality.

STUDIO NEWWORK

A New York-based graphic design studio founded by Ryotatsu Tanaka, Ryo Kumazaki, Hitomi Ishigaki and Aswin Sadha in 2007. Besides working across a range of media spanning print, screen graphics, products and environmental designs, the studio also publishes their biannual large-format arts publication, NEWWORK MAGAZINE.

STUDIOLAV

The young and passionate multidisciplinary design studio looks into different ways of re-interpreting ideas with a playful and ironic spirit by investigating tendencies and curiosity regarding perceptions of form and materiality. Along with expanding their own product collection, they also works on interior design projects and takes on board commissions from a variety of clients.

StudioMakgill

An independent design studio working with businesses and cultural organisations large and small, StudioMakgill focuses on the creation of brand identities and visual communication providing succinct, innovative, beautiful solutions that last, inspire and enable clients to realise their ambitions.

Talmor, Morey

A graphic designer from Tel Aviv, Israel, currently living and working in Brooklyn, New York. His work includes various aspects of design on prints like editorial design, identities, packaging design and illustration.

The Hello Poster Show

Founded by Benjamin K. Shown and Alanna MacGowan in 2009, the Seattle-based fundraising exhibition/program features silkscreened posters created by designers and artists from around the world. Each collection is based on different theme and colour palette.

Therese Sennerholt Design

Beside working on designs for magazines, catalogues, books and visual identities, the art director and graphic designer has also taken a side project to create poster with quotes. The limited edition prints are personal and edgy with a sense of humour.

This Studio

Founded by David Bennett, the UK-based design studio specialises in graphic design, branding and poster design with a strong typographic style.

Tokyo-Go-Go Illustration Studio

Established by illustrator Greg Darroll in 2012, the Durban-based studio provides illustration services and character design for agencies, apparel brands, smartphone applications, products and publications.

TOYKYO

Founded in 2006 upon a shared passion between Mathieu Van Damme and Benjamin Van Oost to spread the happiness by producing beautiful objects and refreshing designs with a dash of fun to the mix, the Belgium-based creative agency is a diverse team specialising in graphic design, product development, set design and advertising concept.

Vayreda, Francesc Moret

Grew up with the northern Catalonia's Olot heritage, Vayreda appreciates timelessness and simplicity of design. He graduated from BAU School of Design Barcelona, and has taken a semester to study at Utrecht School of the Arts in the Netherlands to pursue his love for Dutch design.

Walker, Stewart

A recent graduate from Duncan of Jordanston Art and Design College, Dundee. The London-based graphic deisgner specialises in typography, branding and book design.

Wang, Zhi Hong

One of the most iconic graphic designers in Taipei who experts book design for translated titles. Hong is a six-time winner of Taiwan Golden Butterfly Awards, and international awards, such as Kaoru Kasai's Choice, HKDA Global Design Awards and Tokyo Type Directors Club Annual Awards.

Wudai Shiguo

Breaking into the scene in 2008, the Hong Kong-based branding and advertising creative boutique has made its name for great insight into texture and artistry, with enormous respect to classics and craftsmanship.

Acknowledgements

We would like to thank all the designers and companies who have involved in the production of this book. This project would not have been accomplished without their significant contribution to the compilation of this book. We would also like to express our gratitude to all the producers for their invaluable opinions and assistance throughout this entire project. The successful completion also owes a great deal to many professionals in the creative industry who have given us precious insights and comments. And to the many others whose names are not credited but have made specific input in this book, we thank you for your continuous support the whole time.

Future Editions

If you wish to participate in viction:ary's future projects and publications, please send your website or portfolio to submit@victionary.com